Arts and Crafts of India

ILAY COOPER   JOHN GILLOW   PHOTOGRAPHS BY BARRY DAWSON

ARTS AND CRAFTS OF
INDIA

With 198 illustrations, 134 in colour

THAMES AND HUDSON

To the memory of
Daisy
10.3.1893–13.3.1995
& Magdalena Wieprzec-Babcia
16.5.1916–9.7.1995

ACKNOWLEDGMENTS

Our thanks to: Aboobacker V.C. of Tellicherry and family, especially Saleem C.P., Raschid C.P. and Nadira; Ahmed of Marblekraft, Agra; Dave Altham; Janet Anderson; Tim Applebee; Tim and Ferelith Ashfield; Nick and Julia Barnard; Alan and Karen Beagle; Bradford and Ilkley Community College School of Art, Design and Textiles; Jane Brooks; Diana T. Campbell; Will and Hilary Chester-Masters; A. M. 'Bill' Cooper; Elizabeth De Michelis; Dave Edmonds; Gabriel Photographic Supplies, Bradford; Mary Geddes; S. Gurumurthy and J. D'Souza of Mangalore; Janet Harvey; Alastair Hull; the India Government Tourist Office; the India Office Library; Joel Jaffe; A. Gordon Mendez of Cochin; Bharat and Uma Patadia of Bhavnagar; John Pickford; Rose and Nelson Rands; Al and Susan Roth; Rabi Narayan Sahoo; the School of Oriental and African Studies Library; Bryan Sentance; G.C. Sharma of Churu and family, especially Arvind, Rabu and Ram Ratam (Munji); Alan Smith; John Smith; Bettina Starke; Caroline Stone; Jaidev and Nita Thakore; A. Thomas of Trivandrum; Andrew Vaines; Piers Vitebsky and Sally Wolfe; Goodie and Amrit Vohra; Warrens Photolabs, Leeds; Mary Spencer Watson; Mary Wilson; and especial thanks to Nand Kishore and Sulochana Choudhary of Valsad for their invaluable assistance, and to all the craftsmen across India who were so generous with their time, information and patience.

All colour photographs are by Barry Dawson, except for plates 7, 14, 17, 18, 22, 44, 45, 71, 102, 103, 104, which are by Ilay Cooper. Photographs on pages 2, 14, 21, 40, 61, 63, 74, 80, 131 and 132 are by Barry Dawson, and those on pages 15, 23, 59, 62, 90, 110 and 134 are by Ilay Cooper. All line drawings are by Bryan Sentance.

PREVIOUS PAGE *A Rajasthani craftsman paints faces onto wooden puppet-heads.*

British Library Cataloguing-in-Publication Data

A catalogue record for this book is available from the British Library

ISBN 0-500-27863-6

Printed and bound in Hong Kong by South Sea International Press Ltd

CONTENTS

INTRODUCTION

A thriving creative tradition requires two basic elements: a diverse ethnic mix bringing together the inspiration of a number of cultures, and a wide range of raw materials. The Indian subcontinent offers both: contained within its frontiers is an enormous variety of peoples inhabiting a no-less-diverse physical and climatic environment. Throughout the centuries, as waves of foreigners swept through the land, drawn by the rich alluvial plains, the previous inhabitants retreated into the less-promising hills and scrubby jungles. At the fringes their ideas intermingled. India's climate, ranging from tropical rain forest through arid sandy desert to the eternal Himalayan snows, provided a complete environmental spectrum for the rich variety of animals and plants needed to supply ivory, bone, leather, timber, bamboo and cane; the rock beneath the soil was also rich geologically.

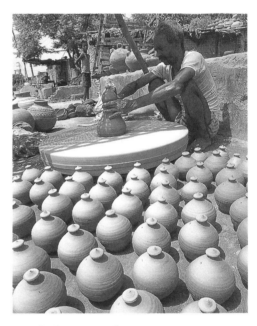

Newly thrown earthenware water pots dry in the sun, in readiness for firing.

The massive diamond-shaped territory that comprises modern India extends south into the ocean and north into the snowy heart of Asia, and projects eastwards to enfold Bangladesh. Geographically, India is divided into five parts: the Himalayan Mountains and their foothills to the north; a broad band south of these foothills, encompassing the extensive alluvial plains of Punjab and the Ganges and Brahmaputra rivers; the Rajasthan Desert in the west; the Deccan plateau – the core of peninsular India – a vast and ancient igneous mass tipped gently east (the Western Ghats plunge to a slender coastal plain on its western margin); and the coastal plain, fringing the Deccan and including much of Gujarat. Partition in 1947, which created Pakistan as a shelter for the Muslims of the subcontinent, tore asunder several cultural entities, such as Punjab and Bengal; consequently any consideration of the cultural background of the region must allow for much overlap across modern political borders.

The overwhelming majority of Indians are descended from Indo-Aryans, peoples who seem to have originated in the Caucasus, spreading across the Iranian plateau through arid Baluchistan or mountainous Afghanistan and entering the rich plains along already well-worn routes. They settled the Indus basin and expanded throughout the Ganges basin, speaking a tongue sprung from the same root as most of those of Europe. They interbred with the native peoples just as later invaders interbred with them. Their languages are current throughout the Ganges basin, Punjab, Assam, Bengal, Rajasthan, Gujarat, Orissa, Madhya Pradesh and Maharashtra. Within this vast area, in the rougher terrain, can be found the older peoples, including the Bhils of south Rajasthan, Gujarat and Madhya Pradesh; the Gonds of eastern Madhya Pradesh; and on the hills to the north and east the peoples of Mongolian extraction – Tibetans of Ladakh, Nepalis, Bhutas, Khasis, Mizos, Nagas and Manipuris (the last three ill-at-ease with the Delhi government). Most of their languages are completely distinct, bearing little relation to Sanskrit. The peoples of Andhra Pradesh, Karnataka, Kerala and Tamil Nadu are Dravidian, one of the pre-Aryan races of India, who, retreating to the south, managed to resist the tides of later invaders – even the Mughals failed to conquer the tip of the peninsula. In their turn, the Dravidian peoples dislodged tribal folk such as the tiny Toda community, known for their characteristic ringlets and handsome black-and-white woven clothes, who cling on in the Nilgiri Hills.

Craft in India, as elsewhere, began with man's attempt to improve upon the natural resources available to him and to make tools to pound, cut or kill. Only the detritus remains, from which we can assemble a picture of a toolmaker crouching, along with his fellows, on some eminence near water, with a view across an often-hostile landscape. From chert, agate or chalcedony, they fashioned axeheads, spear and arrow tips, attaching each firmly to a wooden shaft, probably with leather thongs. From reeds and grass they made mats and basketwork containers. They also noticed that fireside mud solidified in the heat.

With cultivation, the nomadic hunter-gatherer tribes began to settle, and required new tools – ploughs to cut the soil, blades to harvest the crop, and granaries to store the harvest. Communities grew larger and could support individual artisans skilled in some essential craft, and this specialization increased their talents. The people of the Indus Valley, equipped with bronze and copper, moved towards urbanization.

The Indus Valley civilization was the last of three that grew up around the Middle East. Each took root beside a seasonally flooding river which, although good for agriculture, was harmful to buildings. The Egyptians and the Sumerians were the first (fourth millennium BC); and then, in the middle of the third millennium, towns grew up at Mohenjo-Daro and Harappa in the Indus basin. Were the Indus people Dravidians, the last wave of pre-Aryans, later to be driven on southwards? We cannot be certain, but their skeletal remains are very similar to those of the modern inhabitants of the region. Their early pottery evokes that of the Iranian plateau, suggesting that they originated from the west, the way almost all the invaders came, for the snows of the Hindu Kush and the Himalayas were virtually impassable, and the sea bore traders, not invaders. The hills and jungles of the east, meanwhile, had allowed each community to intermingle sufficiently to leave traces on the other without becoming overwhelmed.

The Indus culture covered a large area along the coasts of Baluchistan and Gujarat, reaching far into modern India to the lands between the Ganges and the Jumna. Its outline is traced by common artefacts. Most sites lie in modern Pakistan; those in India include Kalibangan in Rajasthan and the erstwhile port of Lothal, near the Gulf of Cambay.

An urban environment is ideal for cultural advance, for innovation is accelerated by a concentration of people. Towns attract artisans from the hinterland, who come to seek work, patronage or trade, and as they bring new ideas, so they take them elsewhere. The most widespread, if not the most beautiful, creation of the Indus Valley people was the steatite seal. Each was incised into a little tablet – a reverse relief – usually depicting an animal; a bull before a totem was most popular. Above it were hieroglyphs of an undeciphered script. The seals were used to affix the stamp of ownership onto goods.

A Kashmiri potter carrying his work.

Indus artefacts show little connection with those of Mesopotamia or Egypt. Apart from a handful of sculptures, it seems that stone was not much used for decorative or construction purposes. Bronze and copper were widely used for everyday items such as knives, axes, spear-heads or even fish-hooks, but rarely for making figures – the famous statuette of a dancing girl, cast by the 'lost wax' process (see p. 62), is remarkable not only for its beauty.

A floral pattern etched onto black polished clay pottery made in Madhya Pradesh.

Bronze required imported ingredients for its manufacture, and its main component, copper, may have been brought from Rajasthan or Afghanistan – either source would have necessitated secure overland trade routes. There is strong evidence of seaborne trade with Mesopotamia, although only a similarity between the decorative beads of the two regions points to cultural exchange. The Indus peoples may have been exporting textiles, however, for fragments of cloth, patterned fabric incised on figurines, and dyeing vats found among the ruins all indicate that the industry was well established.

Clay was the most widely used material in the Indus basin, where its carefully planned towns were built and paved in brick, a continuing tradition in Punjab and Sind. The potter's wheel was already a familiar item (known to the Sumerians since the fourth millennium BC), turning a variety of vessels specific to the culture: a dish on a stand; a beaker much like that used nowadays for tea on Indian trains; cylindrical, perforated strainers; and a cream-coloured, pointed-based goblet. There were also many modelled pieces, some toys, others votive offerings or even objects of worship, that have close parallels to those produced in modern India.

Time has destroyed much of the handiwork of these people. Little remains of their textiles, leatherwork, basketry or woodwork. That ivory was valued seems implicit in a tragic cameo left in the wake of the final slaughter in Mohenjo-Daro. Beside two tusks lie nine skeletons (five of children), ivory carvers perhaps, caught fleeing with the means of their livelihood. It was the Indo-Aryans who are thought to have given the coup-de-grace to these failing towns around 1700 BC, and they brought few manufacturing skills to rival those they destroyed. It is difficult to tie them to settlements or to artefacts until they were established throughout north India. Their predecessors, overwhelmed, fled southwards before them, or deep into the inhospitable hills and jungles. Was it the Indo-Aryans who, at the close of the second millennium BC, wandered the Ganges basin and left hoards of copper goods in their wake? These included strange anthropomorphic

A contemporary banner made of appliquéd cotton on hessian, depicting a bride being carried in her palanquin (northern Bihar).

sheets of metal, and tools and harpoons which match those that the hunters are wielding in nearby rock paintings. Early in the first millennium BC a new urban society emerged along the Ganges, which was known to archaeologists by its painted grey pottery. By the middle of the millennium iron was in widespread use, and a new style of pottery known as 'northern polished black ware' was prevalent.

The Achaemenid empire of Persia reached the Indus in the 5th century BC, bringing with it the Aramaic script, from which both northern and southern Indian alphabets derive. A new civilization evolved in Bihar and eastern Uttar Pradesh, the names of its cities still preserved in the Hindu epics. Religious speculation was rife, as the Vedic beliefs of the Indo-Aryans, absorbing local ideas and deities, advanced towards modern Hinduism. The 6th century BC gave rise to two great teachers, Mahavir, the founder of Jainism, and Gautama Siddhartha, the Buddha. Two other remarkable men, one a brief intruder, the other an empire-builder, appeared in the late 4th century BC. In 327 BC, having conquered the Achaemenids, Alexander the Great followed the Afghan route into Punjab, only to retreat a few months later by way of Sind. He left Graeco-Bactrian city states behind him, bequeathing India Greek sculptural and architectural styles. About fifty years later, the great Ashoka was expanding the Mauryan empire his grandfather had established in Bihar. He led his people in embracing Buddhism, and built many stupas and monasteries. Craftsmen from moribund Persia were drawn to Pataliputra, his capital, in search of patronage. The site has never been fully excavated but occasionally, beneath the modern city of Patna, architectural fragments are unearthed that display a coupling of typical Persian forms with characteristically Indian features such as a native sensitivity for animals and plants. Most famous of such remnants is the Lion Capital from Sarnath, symbol of the Government of India.

Early in the Christian era the Kushan empire held much of the north-west. Many of the earliest-known images of Hindu deities come from this time, fashioned either from the spotted sandstone of Mathura or Gandharan grey schist. Buddhist sculpture, however, is far more common at both sites, and bears the clear imprint of Greece in both features and clothing.

India was only intermittently ruled as a whole. Even the Kushans were but one of four major powers. The next, and last, northern Hindu empire was that of the Gupta dynasty (mid 4th–late 5th centuries AD), usually seen as the classical epoch. Its sculpture is restrained, realistic and lightly embellished; its sensual, elegant painting survives in some of the Ajanta caves. The poet Kalidas probably belonged to this period.

In the south, the plastic arts reached their zenith during the end of the Pallava period and the Chola period (9th – 13th centuries AD). Some of the finest bronzes ever cast were produced at this time. The figures (generally of deities) are relaxed yet majestic, and charged with dynamism. Many of the finest *nataraja* (portrayals of the dancing Shiva in a circle of flame) belong to this time.

Towards the close of the first millennium AD Hinduism advanced to devour Buddhism, aided as much by the rise of image-worship in the Mahayhana sect as by a priestly ploy that established Buddha as the ninth incarnation of Vishnu. By the 14th century Buddhism was virtually dead in the land that had given it birth. A new challenge had arisen.

Soon after its 7th-century foundation, Islam swept through the Middle East and Iran, forcing many Zoroastrian refugees into India, where, as Parsis, they still retain a separate identity. In the 8th century Islam reached India, taking Sind by sea. The real assault started in 998, when Mohammed of Ghazni descended from Afghanistan in the first of many raids during which he robbed and destroyed towns and temples. His greatest crime in the eyes of Hindu India was the looting and levelling of the great temple at Somnath, on the coast of Gujarat. The temple was perhaps the richest shrine in all India, and he did not neglect to revisit it. The Muslim invaders who followed set up a series of sultanates of varying size, based on the city of Delhi. Centres of Muslim power were established in Malwa and in the Deccan, and gave rise to important kingdoms.

Islam – a faith proclaiming universal brotherhood under God, with Mecca as its earthly focus – may be regarded as the very antithesis of Hinduism. Indian decoration had previously revelled, and excelled, in the portrayal of animal and human forms; both were anathema to Sunni Muslims (although rulers could be cavalier about such strictures). The Sunnis form the great majority of Islam, but the Shias, dominant in Iran and looked upon as heretics by the orthodox, were much more tolerant of figurative art; it is hardly surprising that Persia grew to dominate Islamic art and proved a major influence on painting in neighbouring India. Most of the Islamic regimes that ruled all or part of India were led by Sunnis, although some Shia clans held sway in the Deccan and there patronized painting. But the orthodox also had innovations to offer, introducing a rich vocabulary of abstract geometric and arabesque designs, as well as imposing their own interpretation on the architectural and decorative features that their faith had adopted.

Babur, descendant of both Tamerlaine and Genghis Khan, founded the Mughal empire in 1526 when he invaded India and defeated the last Delhi sultan. His memoirs show him to be an open-minded man, sensitive and curious, who missed the cool, clear air of his native hills. His son, Humayun, lost the empire, only regaining it after a long exile in Persia. He returned with Persian craftsmen in his train; two of these were the painters on which his son, Akbar, was to lay the foundations of a Mughal atelier. Akbar, coming to an insecure inheritance at the age of thirteen, soon put aside his regent to launch the empire towards its greatest achievements. For the next hundred years, patronage was at its most liberal, faith at its most tolerant. For the construction of his new capital, Fatehpur Sikri, Akbar reverted to Hindu architectural forms. Its decoration flew in the face of orthodoxy, with animals, men and even Hindu deities depicted in stone and in paint on its walls. He scandalized the *mullahs* with his free view of religion, and its seeming diversion more towards himself than to God. His half-century reign not only secured but also vastly increased the empire, so that when his son Jahangir acceded in 1605, it was sufficiently stable to allow him to indulge his interest not only in the world of nature but also in painting. He was particularly fond of European art, and foreigners at the court, such as the resident Jesuits, kept him well supplied with pictures.

In 1628 Shah Jahan, a more orthodox Islamic monarch, acceded. He built enthusiastically, and the greatest architectural achievement of his reign was the Taj Mahal. Walls were decorated with abstract or floral designs, and his masons were schooled in the Italian technique of *pietra dura*, which entailed inlaying intricate floral designs in semi-precious stones into white marble. The demands of a

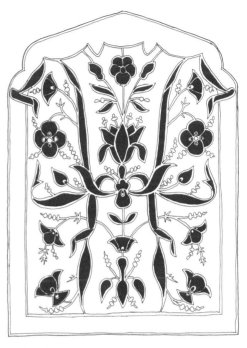

A floral design inlaid in jade on the reverse of a mirror (Mughal period).

wealthy court meant that craftsmanship excelled during this time, producing beautiful jewelry, carved jade, ivorywork, weapons (doubtless as functional as they were decorative), and printed, embroidered and brocade cloths. Meanwhile he built a new capital at Delhi, dominated by the Red Fort and a great mosque, the Jama Masjid. François Bernier, visiting Delhi in the mid-17th century, described its craftwork: 'Large halls are seen in many places called *kar-khanays* or workshops for artisans. In one hall embroiderers are busily employed, superintended by a master. In another you see the goldsmiths; in a third painters; in a fourth, varnishers in lacquerwork: in a fifth, joiners, turners, tailors and shoemakers, in a sixth manufacturers of silk, brocade, and those fine muslins of which are made turbans, girdles with golden flowers, and drawers worn by females so delicately fine as frequently to wear out in one night.'

Had Dara Shikoh, the eldest, free-thinking, and favourite son of Shah Jahan, come to power, the fate of the Mughal dynasty might have been very different, but instead the third son interposed. Puritanical Aurangzeb, able, ruthless and godly, deposed his father and usurped power, slaying his rivals. He settled down to a long reign marred by frequent bloodshed in the Deccan. His intolerance of the infidel, however – the overwhelming majority of his subjects – fuelled rebellion under a Hindu banner. Shivaji, the founder of Maratha power, started an insurgency that was to be the running sore of the empire. Aurangzeb died in 1707, and his son five years after that. Beyond lay decay and disorder.

The principal port of the Mughal empire was Surat, north of modern Bombay, on the Gujarat coast. Here, by hard-won imperial sanction, the foreign traders settled – Persians, Armenians, Arabs, Dutch, Portuguese, French and British, the Europeans anxious for spices and textiles, in particular printed silks and cottons. The native craftsmen were responsive, and adapted their goods to suit their customers' requirements. Trade flourished through the 17th century, but the disorder of the 18th gave the Marathas free rein to advance northwards, isolating the port from the capital, and Surat faded. There were, however, concessions elsewhere. By 1700 the British held the seedling cities of Madras, Bombay and Calcutta, the French had Pondicherry and sites on the Kerala, Tamil Nadu and Bengal coasts, and even the Danes had an enclave. The native powers were fragmented, and as the French had little support from Paris, it was the British East India Company who gained eventual supremacy.

When the wheels of the Industrial Revolution began to turn, trade set about the destruction of the very artisan skills that had in part attracted it. The backbone of India's trading economy was her textile industry, employing huge numbers of skilled spinners, weavers, dyers, printers and embroiderers. Cheap, high-quality machine-produced printed cottons inundated the market in the 19th century. The classic colonial economy developed when, as a result of the suspension of trade with the southern states during the American Civil War, an increasing quantity of raw cotton was provided by India. Tradition still tells how the British 'severed the thumbs' of Bengali muslin weavers. The knife was that same cheap cloth.

The destruction of native industries did not pass unnoticed. During the Indian mutiny of 1857, the last of the Mughal monarchs, Bahadur Shah Zafar, issued a proclamation to the nation which stated that 'regarding artisans, it is evident that the Europeans by the introduction of English articles into India have thrown the weavers, the cotton dressers, the carpenters, the blacksmiths, the shoe-makers etc.

out of employ, and have engrossed their occupations so that every description of native artisan has been reduced to beggary....' Elsewhere, however, the foreigners brought commercial vitality. Kashmir's fine woollen shawls were soon in vogue with the ladies of the chill homeland and production soared. Alien requirements also deflected some craftsmen from more traditional work: for example, the Europeans demanded a whole range of furniture quite unknown to native carpenters. Models and drawings, freely interpreted, gave rise to an entire industry producing colonial furniture. Makers of baskets and stools were soon faced with a growing demand for lightweight furniture in their medium, as fashion expanded the market.

The British brought pictures with them, some of which graced expatriate homes, while others – prints, in newspapers or coloured for decoration – were freely available in the bazaar. Local painters, confronted with this very different way of viewing the world, took readily from the alien idiom, sometimes producing a rich synthesis, as in the Kalighat painting of the early 19th century, but also giving rise to modern Hindu religious kitsch. Only a few rural styles escaped this influence.

In the second decade of the 20th century the Congress Party, led by Mahatma Gandhi, set out to salvage cottage industries. Part of their strategy was a boycott of imported goods, especially textiles, the mainstay of the colonial economy. Instilled in their supporters was a sense of duty to buy and wear *swadeshi* (indigenous) in preference to fashionable *videshi* (foreign) fabrics. The leaders of the movement set the trend by wearing handspun, handwoven *khadi* cloth, and further demonstrated their support for the craftsmen by spinning thread for a certain period each day. Quite apart from his role as a gentle revolutionary, Gandhi was the first politician to concern himself with these issues, which are yet to be better addressed.

Since Independence, disillusionment with political leaders who have hidden their venality behind a swathe of handspun cotton has devalued *khadi*, and the attempt to bring industry back to the village has lost its momentum. Time cannot be reversed, and today the mills of Bombay and Ahmedabad produce excellent, more practical textiles, amalgams of synthetic and natural fibres. Such fabrics as the ubiquitous 'terycot' are far more popular than plain cotton amongst the mass of the populace.

The demand for Indian handicrafts continues to increase in the wealthy Western countries. Along with synthetic textiles, handmade, hand-printed, tie-dyed or batik fabrics are once again major export items, and almost all India's hand-knotted carpets are destined for foreign buyers.

Although many crafts are centred on cities, it is in rural India that they flourish as an integral part of the economy. Some have suffered from the introduction of cheaper, more practical replacements, with moulded plastic imitating traditional materials. Others thrive, unopposed; the earthenware water-pot features in kitchens from Delhi to the smallest hamlet. Most households have a *charpoy* (literally 'four feet'), the wooden-framed bed bound across with handmade twine; often a coarse cotton dhurrie lies across it, perhaps woven by the women of the house. In the chill of northern winter a *rezai* (quilt) is added to the bedding, made up by the local tailor, and other craftsmen walk the autumn streets, plucking the taut string of their bow, the tool of their trade with which they floss out the compacted cotton filling of the *rezai*. The farmer prefers to buy custom-made tough leather slippers in the village bazaar. His wife will choose those covered with hand-embroidery. He may boast a 'terycot' suit hidden away in mothballs, but his workaday clothes are of handwoven coarse white cotton. Her clothes, as long as her husband lives, will be coloured, perhaps locally tie-dyed, or embroidered. After he dies she, too, will assume white cotton.

Many of the villagers' everyday requirements, such as wooden forks and rakes for the fields, axes and knives, iron spatulas and ladles, are village-made, sold by craftsmen in the bazaar. In western India, local encampments of Lohars (tinkers) are often in evidence grouped around their wonderful carts, repairing and replacing metal items, along with the occasional itinerant craftsmen – the repairer of brass pots, the knife sharpener and, ever rarer, the entertainers.

Many crafts are dominated by Muslims, who only comprise some 10 per cent of the total population. Although there is a Muslim elite made up of an aristocracy who either received or took lands from the decaying Mughal empire, and a successful business community, these are a tiny minority. As a whole, the Muslims belong to the poorer section of society, usually landless labourers or tenants of a small tract of land which, even in the good years, barely supports the family. The brassworkers of Uttar Pradesh are mostly Muslims, so are many dyers, including the tie-dyers of western Gujarat. In certain regions, particularly in the south and north-east, Christians form a moderate proportion of craftsmen, and in Punjab and Delhi Sikhs play an important role, whilst in Ladakh the local Tibetan Buddhists predominate. Some communities, such as the Jains and Parsis, are rarely involved with commercial craft except as merchants, but they may display considerable skill within the household. Jain girls from Kathiawar, Saurashtra, are expected to produce fine needlework for their dowries, as are women of other castes.

The layout of each town and village reflects the fundamental structure of society, being divided into Hindu and Muslim *mohalla* (sectors), and these are subdivided amongst castes. Each craftsman, therefore, lives amongst his fellows. The bazaar is divided in the same manner, as the European market once was – with all the cobblers in one section, all the drapers in another.

The distribution of craft production throughout India is often dictated by climate or geography. The supply of any basic raw material is a determining factor, although modern communications have minimized its effect. The humid climates of north-east and south-west India are ideal for the growth of bamboo and the creepers used for cane. Not surprisingly, the best proponents of crafts based on these materials are found there. The ship-building industry relied on access to teak as well as to the sea, and has therefore tended to develop at the mouth of a river flowing from a teak-growing catchment area. Stonework is usually based near the quarries, although sometimes stone blocks are shaped into suitable oblongs to reduce waste before being transported to the nearest town for carving.

Sometimes craft industries are established to ameliorate problems of unemployment, irrespective, perhaps, of the availability of raw materials; this is how the short-lived *bidri*-work of Maharashtra is said to have originated (see p. 60). The brasswork industries of Benares and Moradabad, which were revived by the British, owe their situation more to the concentration of prospective customers than to the proximity of metal mines.

A woman consults a jeweler in his shop in a north Indian jewelry bazaar.

When both raw material and equipment are easily transported a craft may become mobile. Some crafts, such as maintenance skills, are by nature itinerant, although there is always a tendency to settle. Patronage drew skilled jewelers to the new city of Jaipur from the decaying Mughal capital of Delhi during the 18th century and the city's reputation in this regard has blossomed ever since. The precious metals and stones come from all over the world, some landed on palm-lined shores in silent *dhows* on dark nights. The established craftsmen and market, rather than the raw materials, determine Jaipur's success.

By the time of Independence, Indian craft was a mixture of village production dependent on the custom of socially conservative villagers and tribespeople living in comparative isolation from the 20th-century world, urban-based crafts that had catered for the British and the Indian elite, and certain crafts that had become organized as export industries. This situation was to remain virtually unchanged throughout the 1950s and 1960s, as India struggled to cope with and feed its ballooning population and to build up its industries after centuries of destruction wreaked by colonial trade. During this period the state handicraft boards were set up to save craft industries that were on the verge of extinction and to encourage crafts at village level.

A model of a motorcycle, made solely with a pair of pliers and different gauges of wire, by a craftsman in the outskirts of Delhi.

The situation began to change at the beginning of the 1970s, by which stage, with the Green Revolution, India had solved her food problem, and with a policy of economic self-sufficiency was herself producing nearly all the industrial goods she needed. In the late 1960s, a steady stream of foreign tourists embarked upon what became known as the 'hippie trail' to India from Europe via Turkey, Iran, Afghanistan and Pakistan. Idealistic Western youngsters, lured to India by notions of Hindu mysticism, provided an enthusiastic market for Indian craft. They bought, they returned home and enough of them matured into importers and propagandists of Indian craft to keep the export-orientated parts of the industry in business for the next twenty years. At the same time, communications and media spread into the hitherto hardly penetrated interior. This was followed by Bombay cinema, 'Bollywood', with its mix of village pastiche, kitsch mythology and, most importantly, its view of big-city life and big-city fashion, which had a tremendous impact on Indian life. Finally came television and video. Villagers grew increasingly disinclined to buy the customary village-worked craft artefacts, preferring items marketed by large Indian industrial companies and the multinationals. This has led to a decline in craftwork, as it became focused on the less demanding export market and the blander tastes of largely middle-class city-dwellers, whose inclinations are often merely nostalgic. The television is having its deleterious effect on creativity as well. The women of Gujarat, reputedly the world's foremost practitioners of folk embroidery, are now spending much more time watching television than they are embroidering. Their sisters across the border in Sind still have no electricity, so for the moment their embroidery – even finer – is still being sewn.

India is so vast and, for all the homogenizing influences of our age, still so incredibly varied. Caste, religion and local custom are still the basis on which country people live their lives, and although the demand for craft may have in general declined, there are still so many areas where demand is still strong. The innate creativity of the Indian craftsman will respond, possibly with new materials and slight changes of technique, to produce goods of continual appeal. Visitors, urban Indians and the villagers themselves have much to be grateful for.

CHAPTER I

CLAY, LACQUER AND GLASS

A potter at his wheel, while his mate kneads clay. Saurashtra, Gujarat.

Prajapati, one of the titles of Brahma the Creator, who fashioned humankind from clay, is generally synonymous with the word 'potter'– no other artisan can boast a name with such exalted associations. Hindu mythology also furnished the potters with another name. When the god Shiva came to wed his first wife, Sati, they lacked an earthen pot essential for the ceremony; Shiva therefore took two beads from his necklace and made from them a man and woman, the first moulders of *kumbha* (water pots) – potters are therefore also known as *kumbhar, kumhar* or *kumar*.

The plastic arts are ancient, their products brittle but tenacious. The Indus Valley towns were in part constructed of burnt brick, and their ruins are scattered with sherds. One site, Harappa, was quarried by the British for railway embankments, with the consequence that brick some four thousand years old now carries trains across the Punjab. Kalibangan, an Indus town in Rajasthan whose name translates as 'black bangles', was so called because of the broken terracotta bracelets which litter the place. Fragments of pottery — by their colour, decoration and form — are often diagnostic of past cultures, tracing their developments and movements across the land. Yet the pots shown in 5th-century Buddhist murals at Ajanta (Maharashtra) differ very little from those produced today, and the same is true of some of India's earliest earthen toys.

The fragility and bulk of his primary product, the water pot, compels the potter to live as close as possible to his market. All towns and cities, and most villages have their potters' quarter, which is often an extensive suburb. Its buildings are characterized by bulbous walls constructed of rejected pots cemented together and coated with mud and dung. Somewhere in the shade clay will be souring whilst women paint the pots waiting to be fired. Nearby are stacks of fuel, with perhaps a newly opened kiln, a store of finished goods and a couple of donkeys. Donkeys are used to take the pots to market, as they provide the gentlest way of negotiating poor roads. The pots are carried in a pair of tough net panniers laid across the animal's back.

The kiln is usually simple and temporary, often built of broken pots. The craftsmen of Molela, in Rajasthan, make a structure from redundant 'Persian wheel' pots in order to protect their delicate plaques from the collapse of stacked fuel. The fuel varies, according to availability, from wood, sawdust, straw, rice husks and cow-dung to, in some urban areas, a collection of inflammable rubbish. Firing takes three to four hours and the kiln is left to cool slowly. Rapid drying or cooling may cause cracking; therefore in hotter, more arid regions such as Rajasthan the potter works mostly during the winter and the monsoon.

The basic tools of the potter's craft are the wheel, a selection of paddles, and stone 'anvils'. The paddle looks something like a thick, long-handled table-tennis bat, its face hollowed, while the stone is shaped like cottage loaf some 10 centimetres (4 inches) high. Its upper part is used as a grip, and its bottom, which can be either flat or rounded, is held against the inner wall of the pot at the point where the paddle is applied on the outside.

The potter's wheel, probably a Sumerian invention, was familiar to the Indus people. Today, in some places (such as Khanapur in Karnataka), it is raised on a plinth so that the potter stands to work, which is unusual for Indian craftsmen. In Tamil Nadu, where the European-style treadle wheel is gaining popularity, he may sit at a bench to work. The potters of Punjab and Haryana still sometimes use a kick-operated type familiar in the Middle East. The wheel itself may be of stone or, increasingly, cement, but most commonly it is made of clay and donkey-dung, built up on a wooden hub and frame set at ground level. Crouching, the potter slips a baton into a slot in the rim and uses it to spin the wheel, its weight maintaining the momentum. He flops a handful of wet clay onto the hub and effortlessly throws a pot, cuts it away from its base with a taut thread and puts it aside to dry before starting afresh. One marvels at his dexterity and the uniformity of the vessels that dry beside him. It is almost invariably a male occupation. In some parts of the north-east, such as Manipur, the pottery is made by women, but here the wheel is not used. They fashion their work by hand, beating vessels into shape with a paddle and stone.

When the new pot is sufficiently dry to tolerate handling the potter enlarges and shapes it by beating. The result is a thin-walled vessel, its shape characteristic of its area of origin, even of a particular village. It is laid on a soft bed of ash to dry. Usually the body is left its natural colour, but it is sometimes given a red iron-oxide slip or may be covered with a light micaceous clay which fires to a pleasant sparkling fawn. As a rule, women decorate the work, applying a slip, incising patterns and painting rapid motifs in white clay or lime. Decoration varies according to individual and region, from powerful geometric patterns on large vessels made around Pokaran (Rajasthan), to the dashes and scrawls found throughout India.

After firing, some pots are brightly painted for ceremonial use, particularly for marriages. In Bikaner (Rajasthan), special terracotta items were traditionally covered with coloured lacquer and gilt. Glazing is rare, although in parts of Tamil Nadu a blue or green glaze is added to biscuit-ware and in Meerut (Uttar Pradesh) *kashigar* (glazers) buy ready-baked pots and paint them with designs which they then glaze. In Jammu, pots are made that are decorated with a floral pattern on a black ground, and these, too, are glazed, but elsewhere it is more usual for the potter to burnish some of his goods to a fine gloss. The large glazed jars that can still be seen in Gujarat and other coastal areas originated in China and were used to transport opium and ginger.

A painted motif on a black unglazed clay pot, made in West Bengal.

A floral motif decorating cobalt glazed pottery from Jaipur, Rajasthan.

Black pottery is widely manufactured. The technique of blackening varies, but generally involves firing in a closed kiln with some vegetable matter, such as rice husks, strewn amongst the pieces; it is the smoke from this that colours the terracotta. In Nizamabad (Uttar Pradesh) the process is more elaborate: designs are incised on the dry surface and, after firing, are filled with a silver-coloured paint made from a mixture of mercury and zinc. The result imitates a type of metalware known as *bidri* (see p. 60). Some vessels are coated with raw lacquer while they are still hot, which results in a black, glossy, non-porous surface. In eastern Gujarat, where Prohibition reigns, these pots are filled with vegetable extract, raw sugar and water, then buried until the mixture is fermented ready for distillation into the local brew. Excise officers search areas where recent cultivation may conceal such pots and probe the ground with metal rods in the hope of breaking them (a complete earthenware still some 1500 years old is displayed in Taxila Museum in Pakistani Punjab – labelled 'water purifier'!). Small spherical pots are hung beneath newly cut fruit stems of coconut, date or toddy palms to collect the sap, which rapidly ferments into a cider-like 'toddy'.

The fragility of his creations works to the potter's advantage, as there is always a need for replacements. Tradition, too, plays its part in ensuring a constant demand: in Tamil Nadu, for instance, on the day before the harvest festival of Pongal, the clay household vessels are smashed and a spring-cleaned kitchen is restocked with new ones. No factory product yet threatens the traditional water pot, but lighter, less fragile plastic copies are increasingly being used to transport water from the well or pump to the house. The potter has a varied repertoire. There are oval pots designed to lift water for the 'Persian wheel' method of irrigation as well as vases, cups, plates and *lotas* (traditional drinking pots which in Rajasthan may have a spout; the *lota* is rarely taken to the lips but poured into the open mouth). The big, shiny red water jars widely used in south-east Gujarat are built up by hand, beaten into shape with a paddle and stone, and finally burnished with several strands threaded with the dried fruit of the *kachki* tree. Largest of all are the storage jars, hand-moulded and often 2 metres (6 ½ feet) high. These are used for grain, which is released through a stoppered hole in the bottom. They are made from a mixture of clay and cow-dung, built up in situ, course by course, either by a potter or by the householder, and are merely air-dried, as firing would be impossible. Smaller versions are made in the potter's compound and fired. In western Gujarat women often construct their own cupboard of unbaked clay to use as a refrigerator, which they whitewash and decorate with relief motifs and fragments of mirror; relief decoration is common, and sometimes quite intricate. At Chinhat, near Lucknow (Uttar Pradesh), pots are made in plaster-of-Paris moulds, applying a human face in relief to either side, and a moulded water jug made near Honowar (Karnataka) has a spout shaped auspiciously as a cow's head. Until very recently, every hotel room had a small clay water jug or pot: now it is usually plastic.

Mrs Meer Hassan Ali, a resident of Lucknow in the 1830s, sheds some light on the popularity of clay eating vessels from cottage to palace when she mentions that 'many of the delicacies of Asiatic cookery' were 'esteemed more palatable from the earthen flavour of the new vessel in which it is served'. In addition, Hindu tradition frowns on the reuse of such dishes, which are disposable, like the *kulhar* in which syrupy sweets are sold, and railway tea served. As a train sighs out of the station, a certain satisfaction may be gained from hurling one's cup to the ground!

As well as pots and dishes, the potter also makes clay beads, *jhanvan* for cleaning the feet, hookahs and chillums for smoking tobacco (or perhaps something stronger). Architectural elements such as *jali* (trellised screens) and tiles are still sometimes handmade in clay, but *jali* are now being mass-produced in moulded cement, and tiles are lighter and little dearer when factory-made. This has naturally reduced the demand for both, although locally made ridge tiles are still popular. Until the close of the 19th century, Bengali brick temples were beautifully decorated with figurative plaques or bricks depicting not merely deities but also everyday events. These relief pictures were either carved into or applied onto the surface.

A 17th-century terracotta plaque, from Faridpur, Bengal.

Toys and models may also be made from clay. Miniature kitchen utensils are often seen in Gujarati bazaars, particularly in Bhuj, as well as roughly pinched human and animal figures, even wheeled carts. Some, such as the animal and fruit models made in Bengal and Lucknow, are beautifully finished and brightly painted. During the 19th century missionaries introduced a new genre: sets of meticulous little figures illustrating the various castes and occupations of this vast land. Largely moulded, these are still made in several towns including Varanasi (Uttar Pradesh) and Krishnanagar (West Bengal).

Seasonal religious festivals often call for clay images. Some of these are not made by the potter caste. The Gudigars of Karnataka are primarily wood-carvers, but during July and August, in the lead up to the festival of Ganesh, they make clay images of this elephant-headed god. In Maharashtra, where his festival is of great importance, these Ganesh figures, fashioned from unbaked clay, are often very large, but all are doomed to be immolated in water at the end of the festivities. In the Kumartully and Patuapura suburbs of Calcutta, some two hundred families of the Kayasth caste fashion thousands of figures of Durga, Shiva and their four children for the great Bengali festival of Durga Puja. The figure of Durga, a fierce aspect of Shiva's consort, is generally somewhat larger than lifesize, but may even be 6 metres (nearly 20 feet) high. Its skeleton is made up of twisted hanks of straw stiffened with clay, fleshed over with clay mixed with chaff, and finished with fine alluvial clay from the Ganges. The ten hands of the goddess are moulded, but her features are shaped by hand. The images are dried in the sun, then painted over with zinc oxide or whiting. In Rajasthan, April heralds the demand for idols of Gauri and Iser (local forms of Parvati and Shiva); these are for the women's festival of Gangaur, when they will be carried in procession to their marriage. Such figures are, at the climax of the celebrations, immersed in a river or tank, where all the labour that went into their making dissolves into mud.

There are many other local occasions which require fired or unfired clay objects. Prior to Dassehra, in October, the festival that celebrates Rama's setting forth against Ravana, children in western Uttar Pradesh go round extorting money from their elders, carrying a turbaned figure of Ravana and little pierced lamps, all brightly painted. In Kutch, Gujarat, the potter women, who are Muslim, prepare for the same festival by making models of elephants and camels varying from 4 centimetres (nearly 2 inches) to 10 centimetres high, to carry oil lamps. These are usually left plain, but are sometimes brightly painted with poster colours. Not all the seasonal work is figurative: at Diwali, the Festival of Light, Hindus all across northern India buy heart-shaped oil lamps to illuminate houses and streets.

Potters play a major role in the manufacture of more permanent idols for small shrines as well as figures for votive offerings. Demand for the former has been greatly eroded by groups of squatters on the fringes of cities and towns who cast and colour plaster-of-Paris deities turned out from mass-produced rubber moulds. The demand for local gods and votive figures survives. Some Uttar Pradesh potters still make a *kabeez*, a figure guaranteed to appease an enraged deity, and the tribal populace of Bastar (Madhya Pradesh) requires images of folk gods and votive animals, whether of metal or clay, to be heavily overlain with relief designs.

The horse is regarded as an animal of spiritual potency as well as beauty. In Tamil Nadu a terracotta horse, which can be quite enormous, stands guardian at the entrance to most villages. This is Kudirai, the mount of Aiyanar, protector of the community. The legs of the animal are made of clay rolled into four cylinders while the body is built up in stages from clay mixed with sand and straw, to give it more substance. The head is made separately, and supported with pots or pieces of wood whilst it dries in place. These horses are primarily made in Salem and Pudukottai.

Terracotta horses, spiritually significant to varying degrees, are made through much of India. Bankura (West Bengal), Dharbanga (Bihar) and Gorakhpur (Uttar Pradesh) all produce well-known versions. Often they have a red slip and are richly caparisoned with necklets, each jewel being suspended by a wire. The horse is regarded by the Bhil tribals of east and north Gujarat and Madhya Pradesh as a family deity, and Mataji, the mother-goddess, demands its image. Sacrifice is integral to Bhil tradition, and goats and buffalo are slain at Dassehra. Most potters in that region display horses, elephants and leopards made as votive offerings, which are bought to be set up at some sacred site, often in the shade of an ancient tree, and added to over the years. Often there is a small crowd of such beasts, each representing a boon either requested or granted. In the hills east of Surat, in Gujarat, potters make bell-like shrines called *ghummat*, standing about 75 centimetres (over 2 feet) high and constructed in three stages, each course drying in the sun before the next is started. The *ghummat* is finally fired, and when sold will be put at a similar holy site (often carried there in a procession on a cart pulled by bullocks clad in bright saddle cloths), and filled with small votive animals. The form of the larger animals varies regionally, but they are generally made up of eight wheel-thrown elements: four legs, trunk, neck, head and rider, fused together with clay. The smaller beasts are merely pinched into shape, sometimes by the tribals themselves.

In addition to the usual cooking vessels and *chulas* (cooking stoves), the potters at Mariamankovil near Thanjavur (Tamil Nadu) make a large pot with animal heads moulded on at the widest circumference facing the four compass points. These are fired in a U-shaped open kiln, then painted for use at marriages. The women and children make horse and elephant effigies for festivals as well as votive female figures and parts of the body with unfired cow-dung, to be sold at the local temple. These last models are for people seeking miraculous cures.

Molela, near Udaipur (Rajasthan) is justly famous for its plaques, both large and small, which take the form of stelae made up of a sheet of clay about a centimetre thick. This is laid on a board sprinkled with powdered donkey-dung, where it is cut into shape. The deity is then built up of sheets of clay deftly shaped so that a hollow high-relief figure results; the details are all pinched into shape and applied to damped parts of the representation. The finished images are powerful, and lure purchasers from distant villages. A new item in the repertoire is a large stele, perhaps a metre high, on which a jumble of traditional deities are given shape. These are made for the craft exhibition circuit and the drawing-rooms of city-dwellers. The demand for figurative stelae is so strong that potters in Udaipur have started making similar plaques. Clay deities are made in many rural areas, and usually include images of the cobra, which is believed to intercede with the heavens. Panchmura (West Bengal) is famous for such work, and incorporates a model of a shrine, boat-shaped, for the snake-goddess, Manasa.

BLUE POTTERY

Although fine ceramics were greatly valued in India, no attempt was made to establish an industry that could compete with those of Persia and China. Fine Chinese porcelain trickled through the Himalayas in the annual caravans, its price soaring with each breakage; but bright glazed ware came mainly from the west. Persia had first begun to decorate mosques and tombs with colourful ceramic tiles, from where the fashion spread to her neighbours and was carried into the subcontinent by successive waves of Muslim invaders during the 13th and 14th centuries. Multan, now in Pakistan, became a major centre for the production of blue and white tilework and pottery. From here, glazed tiles spread to Delhi, the capital of a sultanate, and thence across the northern Indian plains. Coloured tiles were generally only used to provide relief to sombre stonework. The most beautiful early example, far more ambitious, is the frieze of geese, flowers and banana trees, depicted in greens, yellows and blues, on the east wall of Man Singh's palace at Gwalior Fort (Madhya Pradesh), overlooking the city.

In the early 17th century more intricate tilework was developed in Lahore, now in Pakistani Punjab, the erstwhile Mughal capital. These tiles were a jigsaw of shapes of many colours, comprising figures, flowers and abstract designs. The emperor, Jahangir (1605–27), decorated the north wall of Lahore Fort with such work. During the reign of his son, Shah Jahan (1628–58), the fashion spread to tombs and mosques in the Punjab, but it remained localized: alluvial Punjab is rich in clay but lacking fine building stone, so it was natural that architects should turn to ceramic-work for the decoration of their buildings. The wreckage of an eccentric example – the Chini-ka-Rauza ('tomb of china') in Agra – still remains.

The Mughals brought the fashion for Chinese porcelain to India. Koranic disapproval of silver and gold tableware encouraged wealthy Muslims to use expensive porcelain instead. An indication of the value given to fine porcelain at that time is given by François Bernier, a Frenchman who travelled widely through Mughal India in the mid-17th century. In an account of his travels he describes the palatial houses he visited, mentioning a particular feature: 'Five or six feet from the floor, the sides of the room are full of niches, cut in a variety of shapes, tasteful and well-proportioned, in which are seen porcelain vases and flower-pots.' These were called *chini khana* (china rooms) and were a common element, appearing in

Mughal miniatures and still to be seen in the great Mughal palaces. It was said that in this way a collection of valuable china would not only be handsomely displayed, but any theft would also be immediately apparent from the empty niche.

In spite of the vogue for fine Chinese and Persian porcelain in Mughal times, India made do with its own manufacture of a comparatively crude blue pottery which developed during the sultanate period in Delhi and Uttar Pradesh; Khurja, 70 kilometres (about 43 miles) east of Delhi, is an old centre. In the mid-19th century an innovative ruler, Ram Singh, brought the craft from Delhi to Jaipur, and today Khurja and Jaipur remain the principal producers. Khurja ware is made from a mixture of 25 per cent quartz, 25 per cent feldspar, 30 per cent ball clay, 10 per cent *than* clay and 10 per cent china clay. These proportions may vary: the best china is made with 50 per cent china clay. The liquid mix is poured into plaster-of-Paris moulds. As the water content percolates into the plaster, it deposits a coating of the mixture on the inner surface of the mould. When this is sufficiently thick, the surplus is poured off and the resulting vessel dried, painted and glazed ready for the kiln.

The Jaipur mix usually contains no clay at all. It is made up of 100 kg (220 lbs) of ground quartz, 10–20 kg (22–44 lbs) of green glass, ½ kg (1 lb) of fuller's earth, ½ kg (1 lb) of borax and 1 kg (2.2 lbs) of gum. This is kneaded into a dough, flattened and pressed into an open mould. A vase, for example, will be made up in four parts: a wheel-turned neck; two moulded hemispheres; and a wheel-turned base. The hemispheres are filled with ash or sawdust while they dry, the parts are joined and the surface smoothed over, and the vase is then taken for painting. The outlines are drawn in cobalt oxide using a squirrel-tail brush (little ground squirrels are frequently run over, and the painters collect the tails, from which they make their own brushes). The design is filled in with other metal oxides, each of which is transformed into a bright colour by firing. The oxide of cobalt becomes a deep blue, that of chromium changes to green, cadmium produces a bright yellow and iron oxide becomes a red-brown. The piece is then dipped into a home-made glaze of glass, borax and lead oxide which is made adhesive by the addition of boiled flour. When enough dried pieces have built up they are fired at 800–850°C for six hours in a closed kiln fuelled with charcoal. All the glass melts, but 80 per cent of the quartz is left, and this maintains the form of the vessel. The kiln is left to cool for three days, avoiding any rapid temperature change which so easily cracks the china.

There are several new blue pottery centres, including Chinhat, near Lucknow. All produce similar goods – vases, bowls, plates, jugs, cups, beer mugs, bathroom tiles, door knobs and beads. Most of the output is destined for export.

LACQUER

The lacquer used in China and the Far East is derived from the resin of a tree. Indian lacquer is the protective secretion of a tiny colonial insect (*Tachardia lacca*) which lives on a variety of trees. The resin is harvested four times a year and sent to factories, particularly in Bengal and Madhya Pradesh, for processing. It is used as sealing wax, or it is coloured to decorate woodwork and fashion into items such as bangles. Early European travellers remarked on lacquerwork as one of the features of Indian bazaars. Some Bengal lacquer was used within the state for making cheap items of jewelry such as bracelets and necklets.

A lacquered box, made in Orissa.

In Madhya Pradesh, Ujjain, Rewa and Indore all produce lacquerwork, but the demand has faded with the onslaught of plastics. Dahod (Gujarat) was an important bracelet-manufacturing town, but the industry there is now almost extinct; in Hyderabad (Andhra Pradesh), however, not far from the famous Charminar monument, many Muslim craftsmen still use lacquer to decorate bangles. The basic shape is crafted either from glass or from a light golden alloy. Coloured lacquer is applied, molten, to the outer surface and set with small, bright pieces of glass and gilded shapes. Fatehpur, Shekhawati (Rajasthan), is one among many small towns where bangles of pure lacquer are still made. Most of the artisans are Muslims, often women, who can deal more easily with female customers. These lacquer workers buy in processed lacquer, some of it coarse, brown and almost clay-like in appearance. The rest is fully refined and translucent, purchased ready-dyed or to be coloured by the bangle-makers. They heat it, flatten it out and sprinkle cloth dye over its surface. It is then kneaded with a rounded stone until the colour is well mixed.

A woman bangle-seller in a market in New Delhi, sorting glass bangles.

Bangles are made in small bazaar shops in front of the customer. Sitting cross-legged before a small, cement-lined box containing burning charcoal, the woman heats some coarse lacquer on a short wooden rod until it is sufficiently malleable to be rolled into an elongated cone about 10 centimetres in length. She then heats a fine coloured lacquer, applying it over all or part of the cone, depending on how many colours she is to use. When she is satisfied with the colours, she rolls out the cone with a wooden tool, T-shaped in section, called a *hatha*, so that it becomes long and snake-like in shape. As she rolls, she may twist it so that the lines of colour form a spiral. She then uses the heated *hatha* to press the length of lacquer into a wooden mould before joining the two ends into a bangle. This is heated again and run over the groove in the mould, particularly where it is joined. The bracelet is then put onto a blunt-ended cone-shaped wooden implement to ensure that the shape is a true circle, as well as to set the size, since it can be enlarged by heating and pushing it further onto the cone.

There are many ways of altering the colour patterning or decorating the bangle. Sometimes a spiral of thin gilded ribbon is run the length of the warm lacquer, causing it to bulge away from the constriction. This ribbon sets into the lacquer, as do the many different types of mass-produced decoration that are used to add sparkle to the finished bracelet.

Lacquer is also used for decorating wood and brass, and is fashioned into beads, brooches and hair ornaments – particularly in Madhya Pradesh and Bengal. The industry is now shrinking, however, as cheaper, more durable substitutes establish themselves on the market.

GLASS

Glass is made and blown in several regions of India, but nowhere rivals Firozabad, in Uttar Pradesh, where glass is manufactured and processed to feed smaller industries across the subcontinent. This is the capital of what must be the world's largest bangle-making industry. The town's crowded streets are full of little cycle-wheeled *lari* (barrows) laden high with strings of brightly coloured bangles that are proceeding to the next stage of their decoration. Most Indian women wear them and, traditionally, those worn by a bride will be smashed on her wedding night.

Although the industry in Firozabad is now generally housed in large factory sheds, it has not yet been mechanized. The craft is dominated by Muslims. When India was partitioned a number of local families migrated to Pakistan where they set up a parallel industry (now second only to that of Firozabad) in Hyderabad, Sind, which has largely been mechanized. Firozabad will soon follow suit.

Within dark sheds figures move purposefully, each bearing an iron rod, hooked at the end. On many of these a red-hot 'aubergine' of glass is attached. There are usually two circular furnace complexes. In one of these the glass is made. This has white-hot openings giving into vats of molten fluid, some colourless and some coloured to the batch requirement (often scarlet). A worker comes to an aperture, sinks his rod into a vat of white glass, twists it, and draws it out with some of the glass adhering to the rod. This cools slightly before he inserts it again until a reasonable quantity of glass has built up. Then, wielding it high to avoid burning his workmates, he carries it to another aperture to give it a coat of coloured glass. The principle is therefore similar to that used in lacquer bangle manufacture in that the bulk of the object is made up of cheap material, and only the outer layer is coloured.

The loaded rod is carried to the second furnace where the glass is re-heated and shaped to an approximately square section running to a pointed tip. The rod is then handed to the master-craftsman who sits in front of his own small furnace, through which runs a long iron shaft. At one side of the furnace a man turns a handle, rotating the shaft. The master introduces the molten glass, touching the tip against the shaft, to which it adheres. As the shaft rotates it extracts a thread of glass which, by careful continuous movement, the master runs along the shaft in a tight spiral. Considerable skill is needed to keep the movement regular, producing a 'spring' of glass, and the thread to a uniform thickness.

When one rod-load of glass is exhausted, the handle-turner pushes the shaft forward so that the far end projects at the opposite side of the furnace. There, the completed spiral of glass can be removed – it merely slips off – whilst another piece of molten glass is applied to the section of shaft still in the furnace.

The tight springs of coloured glass are taken outside to a yard where men using diamond blades cut down the edge of the spiral so that it becomes a collection of open bangles. These are strung into garlands of 312 and are taken to be fused and hardened by baking. When they have cooled, some will be patterned with nicks cut into the outer surface by a rotating corundum wheel. As each consignment is completed, it is loaded onto a *lari* and taken away to another factory, perhaps in another city, where each bangle will be decorated with golden paint or bright glass 'jewels'. They are then distributed throughout the country or else exported.

The glass industry in Firozabad is not confined to bangle production. At other factories men blow glass, mostly for decorative items, and also shape ornate chandeliers and similar items for urban drawing-rooms. Some units make small glass animals, a fashion imported from Europe. Both coloured and plain glass is supplied to other industries across the country. The ingredients come from all over the subcontinent: soda ash from Punjab and Bombay is mixed with sand from northwest Rajasthan at a proportion of about 9:20. Arsenic is added to clear the glass, then the colouring agent is added – silenium for scarlet, for example.

India has a long and distinguished history of making glass beads, both for the local and export markets. Its fame as a bead-making centre was primarily based

A craftsman making glass-bead samples for cottage-industry workers to copy, in Varanasi, Uttar Pradesh.

on the country's abundant and accessible supplies of a wide range of semi-precious quartz materials – chalcedony, agate, onyx, jasper and rock crystal, although by 1000 BC glass beads were being made in north India. Small drawn-glass beads, used in beadwork, were a speciality, and in fact seem to have originated in India. These were carried to East Africa and South-East Asia throughout the first millennium AD. The main centres of production were Brahmapuri and Arikamedu in southern India. By the 16th century the Indian bead-making industry was sorely hit by competition from the increasingly industrialized products of Venice and Germany, and fell into steep decline.

Bead-making has revived in modern times. Firozabad supplies the glass. At nearby Purdalpur are made copies of Venetian millefiori beads. Papanaidupet, in the south, manufactures drawn-glass beads and glass beads in the Czech style are made in Varanasi. The several large bead 'factories' of Varanasi are, in effect, warehouses from which glass is distributed to the cottage-manufacturers and to which the completed beads are returned for packing and despatch, for the output is entirely export-oriented. It is in the factory, however, that samples are made to be sent out to the major buyers. Most of the rods of coloured glass used in the process are made in Firozabad but some varieties, such as the sparkling one they call 'goldstone', which contains metal dust, are imported from Italy.

The worker sits at a table with, in front of him, a row of six little wicks fuelled by paraffin. A fan of brass tubes, pointing one toward each wick, curves back and down to join into a single pipe leading to a foot pump on the floor. When the wicks are lit, the air from the tubes blows the six flames towards a focal point where the heat is sufficient to melt glass. One foot pump is able to feed ten such arrays of tubes.

To make the beads, the craftsman holds a rigid wire coated with china clay, resembling a sparkler, in his left hand; in his right he has a rod of coloured glass which he melts in the focused flame. He applies the glass to the red-hot wire, forming a rough ball which he then rolls in a mould to produce the required shape. Onto this basic bead he adds other colours of glass in a pattern. One bead completed, he repeats the process some 2 centimetres along the wire until he has completed four or five large beads. He then stands the wire, flower-like, in a small pot, takes up another wire and continues his work. When he is ready he dips the wires into water. The china clay dissolves and the beads slip easily off.

The crafts dependent on clay and glass are still flourishing. The earthen water pot remains an essential feature of every Indian household. The porosity of terracotta feeds the evaporation so vital in keeping the water cool, and this characteristic is unsurpassed by any factory product at a competitive price. The increasing popularity of the light plastic pot to carry water home from the nearest pump, tap or well does, however, drastically cut demand; it is during this frequent journey that most pots are finally broken.

Constant breakage, particularly of the ubiquitous bangles, also keeps the glass craftsmen busy, but their employment is threatened by mechanization. Thanks to a lively overseas market and a growing indigenous middle class, the blue pottery industry remains buoyant. It is the crafts using lacquer that are in most danger; modern acrylics have replaced coloured lacquer for decorating many wooden items, while plastic can be used in the mass production of objects previously made wholly of lacquer.

1 RIGHT A terracotta plaque of Dharamraj, a heroic folk deity, made by a potter from Molela, south Rajasthan. Traditionally these plaques are painted in bright primary colours and used in local shrines.

2, 4 RIGHT *Female and male figurines made of baked clay, from Midnapore district, West Bengal.*

3 BELOW *A terracotta toy boat from Goalpara, Assam. The pinched facial features and large ears of the figures are derived from traditional depictions of the goddess Shasti.*

5 OPPOSITE, BOTTOM *A terracotta festival lamp in female form, from Madras.*

6 OPPOSITE, RIGHT *A pottery votive horse from Gorakhpur, Uttar Pradesh. The potter makes the animal, but it is left to the womenfolk to add the decorative designs.*

7 ABOVE *Large earthenware water jars stacked for sale, in Buhari, Surat district, Gujarat. These pots are built up by hand rather than wheel-turned.*

8 LEFT *A painted pot from Bhuj, Kutch, in Gujarat. This style of pottery is produced by Muslim potters all over Kutch. Their wives paint on the designs with colours obtained from red and white clay and black pigment before the pots are fired in an open kiln.*

9 RIGHT *A terracotta figure of a Brahman bull, from Dhubri, Assam.*

10 LEFT *A display of glazed painted plates for sale outside a shop in Jaipur, Rajasthan.*

11, 12 ABOVE *Ceramic glazed tiles from Jaipur.*

13 ABOVE RIGHT *Vases from Jaipur. Jaipur blue pottery contains no clay. It is turned or moulded from a mixture of quartz, green glass, borax, fuller's earth and gum, then painted with metallic oxides.*

CHAPTER II

STONE AND WOOD

Among man's earliest crafted objects were those made from stone or wood – a fragment of stone or a branch of convenient shape taken from the surrounding detritus and adapted more completely to the task in hand. Hard, siliceous minerals were chipped into blades, and stones into grinders and beaters, while branches were shaped for handles, rods and clubs. The chipped blade industry faded with the rise of metal, but stone continued to be worked for domestic implements, carved or lathe-turned for decorative as well as utility items. Carving and lathe-turning were equally useful for exploiting the rich range of timbers. India's dense forests were barely scratched by the then tiny human population, but with extraordinary rapidity the species spread, the numbers grew and the forest was laid low. Timber, carefully husbanded, can be replaced, however; the mineral resources, although vast, are finite.

STONE

Although tools of chert and chalcedony can commonly be found in amongst the ruins of the ancient Indus civilization, there is little worked stone. The sculpture that has been recovered – a fine bearded head (probably of a priest) and a lovely recumbent ibex – exhibits no lack of skill, however, and may have been crafted by ivory-carvers as a sideline. There are also soapstone seals, which are so finely carved and their animal motifs so expertly executed that they seem more like items of jewelry. The favourite image, incised in reverse relief, was a broad-chested standing bull with great, sweeping horns, facing a totem. Already the Indian mastery of natural form is apparent.

Stone features prominently in the art and architecture of ancient Persia, Sumeria, Assyria and Egypt, but India stood aloof until the Mauryan rulers centred in Bihar started to use carved stone. The Lion Capital of Sarnath (2nd century BC), its form Persian, its lions Indian, which is now the symbol of the Republic of India, dates back to this period.

Alexander left in his wake Hellenic city-states in the north-west that gave rise to an Indo-Greek style of sculpture in Gandhara (north-west Pakistan) and Mathura (western Uttar Pradesh), which became the vehicle of a new faith – Buddhism. In the early centuries of the Christian era, however, Hinduism emerged out of the Vedic beliefs and stone became the preferred medium for depicting its gods. The Gupta rulers (4th–6th centuries) presided over a classic era of Indian sculpture and restrained images of the supreme deity, simply clad, became numerous. In the south, the great epoch for sculpture came under the Cholas (9th–13th centuries). Sculptors carved not only freestanding figures but also great masses of living rock.

14 LEFT *Wooden brackets, exquisitely carved from local teak, supporting the projecting upper storey of an old house in Ahmedabad, Gujarat.*

Stone became the accepted medium for religious architecture and sculpture within a faith richly endowed with physical manifestations of a godhead. From the 11th to the 14th centuries many temples were built in central and northern India. There are some wonderful examples, such as the Khajaraho temples (Madhya Pradesh, 11th century), the Sun Temple at Konarak (Orissa, 13th century, about which Murray's Guide for 1931 warns: 'unhappily much of the decoration is of a licentious character'), and the breathtaking delicacy of the marblework of the Dilwara Jain temples at Mount Abu (Rajasthan, 12th century).

Islam, in contrast, traditionally frowned upon the depiction of man and beast, but decoration was not neglected; it was Shah Jahan who introduced the Italian craft of *pietra dura* – the inlaying of semi-precious stones into marble, which still thrives in Agra, the city of the Taj Mahal. The craftsmen, exclusively Muslim, decorate marble plates, wall plaques, boxes and bowls, which are mostly made beside the Makrana quarries of Rajasthan. They employ an ever-extending vocabulary of floral motifs, each represented by a little collection of brass templates. The work is extremely taxing. Every tiny petal, section of leaf or even stamen is made from a separate stone. The craftsman breaks off a fragment of thinly carved stone and proceeds to shape it, holding it against the appropriate brass template – a petal shape, perhaps. He applies it to the abrasive edge of a vertical wheel operated by a bow (its leather thong looped around the axle), and grinds the stone fragment down to match the brass shape. The pieces of leaf are often assembled, stuck together with lacquer, before it is shaped. Flowers are always worked petal by petal, and can have from ten to a hundred parts. The stones used include deep blue Afghani lapis lazuli, green African malachite, red carnelian from Gujarat and Iranian turquoise, along with Bengali mother-of-pearl.

Stone inlay work, Agra.

The pieces are laid upon the surface to be decorated, and their outlines traced onto it with a fine scribe. The segments of each element of the design are then piled separately on a tray and the craftsman cuts out the recesses with a small chisel, using a little iron bar as a mallet. When complete, these are filled with a light cement that melts when the surface is heated, and before it sets again the fragments are eased into place. Only plant stems, delicate and vulnerable, are shaped after their recesses have been cut. Finally, the surface is burnished with emery stone and jeweler's polishing powder.

In a land so steeped in idolatry, sculpture thrives. Freestanding figures, almost invariably gods, continue to be carved in many parts of the country, sometimes in strict conformity with the *shilpashastra* (the ancient code governing the aesthetics of stone-carving) but often more freely. The market extends out to expatriate Hindu communities spread throughout five continents. The heart of this industry, by sheer output, lies in the south-west quarter of the walled city of Jaipur. White Makrana marble arrives in roughly shaped blocks, to be cut up by drilling a row of holes and hammering iron wedges into it until the stone breaks along the line of weakness. This drilling was done by hand using a hammer and a bladed rod, but electric drills are now taking over. Diamond-tipped chisels and electric grinders have improved the mason's lot, and their noises now compete with each other along the narrow streets.

In the crafting of these figurines, a man will work from a vertical axis drawn down the roughly formed statue, continually outlining the parts he is to work. Any breakage of a god's body makes it useless for worship. The finished image is brightly painted with acrylic colours. Large idols are produced to order, but smaller carvings of the ever-popular Ganesh, Krishna and Rama are constantly turned out. Lintels, pillars and arches for temples are also in regular demand. An increasing amount of work is done in Makrana itself, beside the great man-made chasm from which even the marble for the Taj Mahal was dug.

By the main roads on the fringes of a number of cities and holy places in Uttar Pradesh, settlements of carvers have grown up, comprising low-caste Hindus. They carve large figures, up to 2 metres (6 ½ feet) in height, from buff Mirzapur sandstone. Hanuman, the monkey-chief of Hindu mythology and devoted helper of Rama, is a popular subject, but there are also smaller, oddly proportioned images of the bespectacled Independence hero Dr Ambedkar, who, long dead, presides over the gradual political rise of his fellow 'untouchables'. Within some cities such as Varanasi there are still Brahmin sculptors producing smaller sacred figures, whilst dealing in the larger ones. Stone for a principal temple deity is selected with care, for its markings and colour must be judged auspicious. Some *sthapathi* (sculptors) will fast for a day, then worship Ganesh, lord of beginnings, before starting work. This inspires the deity to enter the stone, guiding the mason's hand.

A sandstone latticework jali *screen, carved in Rajasthan in the late 19th century.*

South India, too, has a rich sculptural tradition, but it is still caught in the shadows of the classical Chola epoch. Mamallapuram, in Tamil Nadu, a town boasting fine stone monuments, has become the focus of granite carving through a school set up by the government in 1957. Here, from black granite extracted from quarries near Kanchipuram, deities up to 6 metres (nearly 20 feet) in height are created, following the dictates of the *shastras* in various southern styles. The hardness of the stone means that the carvers need to temper their steel chisels regularly. They belong to the Vishwakarma community, like many others in the south. The industry is encouraged by the southern preference for granite idols in temples.

There are a number of carving centres in Andhra Pradesh (Durgi, Alagadda) and Karnataka (Shivarapatma, Nagamangala and Karkala). In Karkala grey granite images are worked in conformity with the *shastras*. These dictate that the height of a deity should be divided into ten *tala*, each section of the body in fixed proportion to the others. A *tala* should consist of twelve *angula*, except for the face (from forehead to chin), which has thirteen. A replacement idol must reproduce the original, but be a fraction larger. The image acts as a form of spiritual conductor: the flow of too much power will damage a less exalted soul, so three varieties are made that differ in spiritual potency. The most powerful is intended for a Brahmin household, that for Rajputs and Banias is less spiritually charged, while the weakest is made for the Sudras. An important sideline in Karkala is the *nagakalla* ('cobra stone'), a stele with one or more cobras, or a cobra with several heads, carved in relief upon it. Such stones are widely made in India and are intended to intercede with the deity. In Karnataka they are often set up under a tree or by water to bring fertility to the childless, or even to obtain relief from venereal disease.

At Kesaria, in southern Rajasthan, a dozen families are employed in the craft. They work dark chlorite and soapstone from quarries in the vicinity, filling a little street near the ancient Rishabdev Temple with the sound of steel on stone. Here, too, the snake stones are manufactured, as they are in Molela, 100 kilometres (about 62 miles) to the north, although there they are fashioned in terracotta. In addition to the major gods, local deities are also carved. Bhil tribals come here from distant villages to buy memorial stelae, made from local soapstone. Relatives of the deceased choose the image they feel most appropriate: the most popular for a man is a rider on horseback, sword in hand, or a man on foot bearing a bow and arrow. A man with joined hands commemorates someone who died in worship, whilst a woman with a baby marks a death in childbirth. Until recently, these carvings were left with a smooth matt finish, but now they must be vividly painted – a fashion, so the cutters say, imported from Jaipur.

Soapstone, which is found in a number of places in India, is used for making small items and tourist souvenirs. As it is soft, it can easily be carved into decorative elephants, boxes and bowls, some of them inlaid, such as those produced on a large scale in the Gokulpura suburb of Agra and in several parts of Varanasi. Other soapstone artefacts are more utilitarian (ash trays, cups, bowls, vases and even conical chillums for smoking hashish), many of them turned on a hand lathe in Jhansi, a town near an important source of the stone in Uttar Pradesh, as well as in Gaya (Bihar), Puri, Bhubaneshwar and Lalitgiri (Orissa) and in the Manbhum and Singhbhum districts of West Bengal. Soapstone is so soft that it can be cut with a handsaw and shaped with a chisel – no mallet is needed.

WOOD

Timber is India's most threatened resource, owing to the gulf between a government policy of conservation and replanting, and its implementation. Nevertheless, a variety of trees survives: the deodar and walnut of the Himalayan foothills; teak, sandal and ebony of the Western Ghats; and the widespread *shisham*. But of the great forest that surrounded the first agriculturalists, mere fragments remain.

Craftsmen exploited timber for its strength and for its potential as a carving medium. Their skill blossomed throughout the 19th century as feudal rulers, long the major patrons, were eclipsed in this role by business communities which, in a century of unparalleled peace, flourished on imperial trade. They devoted vast sums to ostentatious building and their projects attracted concentrations of craftsmen, including carpenters. Beautiful carved facades and interiors stand as their epitaph.

Decorative timberwork is widespread. In Punjab beautiful wooden balconies can be seen, enclosed by pierced screens, and to the north, in Kangra (Himachal Pradesh) houses are often decorated with bas-relief carving. Carpenters drawn to the Rajasthani district of Shekhawati by the meteoric rise of local merchants established a reputation for themselves with their doors, door-surrounds, carved beams and little shutters. The mansions of rich merchants of Chettinad, north-east of Madurai (Tamil Nadu) include carved columns, capitals, brackets, beams and lintels. Doors may be 5 metres (16 ½ feet) high with relief panels depicting deities, especially Lakshmi, goddess of wealth, patroness of business folk. In Kerala, in the shadow of the richly forested Ghats, craftsmen produced wonderful sculptured woodwork in temples, palaces and great houses, alive with full-relief deities and demons. The brackets supporting projecting balconies and floors of Gujarati mansions were deeply carved totems of intricately interwoven, struggling animal forms, an orgy of life quite at odds, it seems, with the ordered world of an orthodox Hindu householder. Carved screens keep the interior secret but airy; beams and pillars are decorated and on the main lintel Ganesh, lord of wisdom and beginnings, presides over the entrance. In amongst the houses there may be a

A carved window frame, Kashmir.

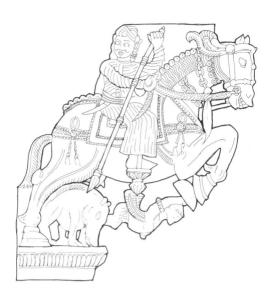

A carved wooden bracket depicting a nobleman boar-hunting, from Kerala.

kabutarkhana (a pigeon house) to attract the holy birds. Mansions such as these were constructed well into the 20th century and survive in the merchant *mohalla* (sectors) of larger towns.

When stone was in short supply, religious buildings were made of timber. Kashmir has fine wooden mosques, and the steep-roofed pine temples of north Himachal Pradesh often bear relief figures on their outer walls. In Goa the Portuguese employed local carpenters to make high-relief altarpieces, screens, furniture and statuary for the churches of their Indian empire. Gilded cherubs still flutter across ceilings and around pulpits in the churches of Goa, Daman and Diu.

The demand for carved woodwork declined sharply during the 20th century. Now the old work is sought after, torn out of rented houses to supply much-coveted decorative items for the urban and foreign drawing room. There is still a market for new doors and door-surrounds in hotels, temples and mansions, however, both within India and abroad, keeping carpenters busy in coastal Karnataka, Coimbatore and Salem (Tamil Nadu) and Tirupati (Andhra Pradesh).

In southern India, many temples keep huge processional chariots to be pulled by the faithful, which can measure up to 15 metres (nearly 50 feet) in height. These are covered with carved figures of guardians, mythical beasts and deities appropriate to the temple's god. Most famous are those of the Jagannath Temple at Puri (Orissa), which gave rise to the word 'juggernaut'. These processional cars are still being made in Orissa, Andhra Pradesh, Tamil Nadu, Kerala and Karnataka.

Early European visitors to India were struck by the dearth of furniture in mansions and palaces. Chairs, when used, were raised little above the floor – carpets, dhurries and bolsters were provided for sitting on or against. The Portuguese thus commissioned copies of their own furniture, which the carpenters decorated with considerable freedom, combining Eastern and Western styles. Later the French and British also commissioned furniture, and the alien forms took root. During the 19th century, heavy furniture of densely carved ebony was widely made in the south (eventually replaced by rosewood as ebony became rare). In Kashmir deeply carved walnut furniture is a speciality. Despite fine craftsmanship, the decoration of modern furniture, aimed at the nouveau riche, is often impractical and ugly.

Ivory inlay was popularized by Muslim patrons so that many of the patterns are geometric, incised into the wood and filled by appropriately shaped pieces of ivory; generally, the wooden articles were made by Hindu Vishwakarmas whilst the inlaying was done by Muslims. The finest example of such work embellishes the doorway of Tipu Sultan's tomb at Srirangapatna (Karnataka) built in the early 19th century. The technique – transformed – thrives particularly in Mysore. With ivory now banned, bone and, more commonly, plastic, replace it, set in a matrix of dark rosewood. The modern work is more marquetry than traditional inlay, with varicoloured woods used along with ivory substitutes to produce pictures, often religious, from mass-produced 'maps'. Marquetry is common in Kerala and coastal Karnataka, a byproduct of the plywood factories. In Surat, too, a few men are still making little marquetry boxes.

Tarkashi is another form of inlay practised in Uttar Pradesh. At Mainpuri, once a major centre, a single family maintains this craft. Onto a plain dark *shisham* surface, a *naqsha* (map) of the design is glued. The outline is then incised into the wood with a little chisel. The worker cuts 2-millimetre ribbons from a sheet of brass, tempers them and then, placing one on edge in an incised line, he hammers it until it is flush with the surface. The brass comes in several gauges, the thickest being used for strong outlines, the finest for details such as hair. The surface is finally polished and varnished. Originally, *tarkashi* work was used to decorate *khadaun*, which are wooden sandals worn by pious Hindus.

Lathe-turned elements of furniture, wall pegs, utensils and toys are often decorated with coloured lacquer. Concentrations of this lacquerwork can be found in Jullundur and Patiala (Punjab), Patna (Bihar) and Sankheda (Gujarat) but the craft, although declining with the adoption of acrylic paints, is still widespread. The main woodcraft of Sankheda used to be architectural carving for buildings, but when rising labour costs killed this industry, the carpenters turned to lacquer-work, which now employs some 150 households. They make chairs, rocking chairs, sofa sets, tables, babies' cots and walking frames, mostly from teak. Both men and women paint. First a thick coat of colour is applied (often mauve), on which a design is created using silver paint made from alloy hammered into thin foil then ground up with glue. When it is dry, the piece is put in a bow-operated (or increasingly mechanical) lathe and rotated over a bowl of glowing charcoal whilst the surface is smoothed with an agate. Then, an orange stick of lacquer is applied in approximately 30-centimetre sections, which melts onto the hot surface and is rubbed over rapidly with an oiled *kevra* leaf. The orange lacquer virtually blackens the mauve but the silver design glows through, golden. Flat surfaces are heated and lacquered section by section. Elsewhere, several layers of lacquer, each a different colour, are applied then cut in patterns to a variety of depths, thus exposing the range of different colours.

Wooden boxes and chests were once major dowry items, but have now been replaced by metal cupboards and trunks. Bhavnagar (Gujarat) is known for its *patara*, a bridal chest on wooden wheels. Once, it held at least eight cunningly concealed compartments for valuables and, reinforced by decorative iron and brasswork, weighed 4 maunds (80 kg, or 176 lbs). Today, outmoded, it is shabbily made of rough *sajad* wood covered with thin galvanized sheet metal that may sometimes even be salvaged from canning factories, complete with bright pictures and brand names, and brass-looking anodized steel. Spectacular boxes often have nuptial associations. The craftsmen of Kerala, for instance, still make an oblong chest with a rounded lid, a small, almost spherical 'Malabar box' for cash and, most famous, the handsome *naturapetty*, nine-sided, with its lid rising like a ridged roof. All these boxes are usually made of wood from the jackfruit tree, reinforced with brass hinges and brackets and finely painted on a vermilion background. Sometimes rosewood is used for the *naturapetty* and its surface merely varnished, as sufficient decoration is provided by the look of the brasswork against the dark wood. The box holds a bride's valuables, but there is also a compartment for betel and the tools and spices associated with it. These are offered at the wedding, giving the guests a chance to glimpse inside. In Kashmir, the bride's jewel case is of walnut carved in high-relief. Raghurajpur (Orissa) is noted for its *jantaka pedi*, a dowry box covered with pictures from Hindu myths. More commonly, chests are decorated with relief carving, such as those made in Chamba (Himachal Pradesh) for storing grain. In Ladakh storage chests are brightly painted with Tibetan Buddhist motifs. Many artisans specializing in weapon-engraving lived in Nagina, in Uttar Pradesh, until the production of weapons was banned after the Mutiny (1857–8), whereupon they turned to ebony carving.

A wooden head of Bhima, one of the heroes of the Mahabharata, *carved and painted for a festival in southern India.*

Certain occupations demanded special containers: writers needed boxes, often beautifully painted, for pens, and others for loose leaves of manuscript (Patan, in Gujarat, and Bikaner, Rajasthan, were renowned for both). Technology has consigned them to the museum. Smallest are the conical nose-ring boxes and *sindura* – painted or lacquered jars to hold *sindur*, the scarlet powder with which a married Hindu woman marks her parting and which is first applied after marriage by the groom. In the Udaipur region (Rajasthan) a box with a carved peacock on its lid is used for the rice, *sindur* and sugar needed to mark the forehead at festivals, and at times of arrival and departure.

Sculptors, like many craftsmen, tend to collect in large towns, particularly religious centres where wealthy pilgrims provide an important market. Around Tirupati small wooden images of Venkateshwar, whose temple dominates the town, are made from red sanderswood. The sculptor uses separate chisels, each named, to form the eyes and ornaments. Temple work is often allotted to a specific community of carpenters. The temple idol is the godhead himself, but those for household worship are less spiritually charged. Unlike most processional figures, the deities of the Jagannath Temple at Puri are replaced annually, the wood coming from a *neem* tree bearing natural marks on its trunk relating to Vishnu (a conch or a quoit, perhaps). In contrast, figures of Gauri and Iser, commonly carved at Bassi, near Chittor (Rajasthan), may be treasured from year to year.

Caste skills are usually passed on from father to son, but there are now training centres open to everyone. At Mamallapuram (Tamil Nadu) woodwork is taught as well as stonecraft, and in Andhra Pradesh, at Kalahasti, is a temple that has attracted a concentration of carpenters who make freestanding deities, some framed with pierced woodwork, and figurines of horses. At Trivandrum and Cherpu (Kerala) intricate figures in rosewood are worked for export or for the drawing-rooms of the rich. Carved elephants, once made of ebony, are a speciality of Kerala; those of Trichur are praised for their realism.

Unique to a small area of Karnataka are *bhootha* figures, totems in the shape of standing men, some almost 6 metres (20 feet) high, men on horseback and a variety of animals, including pigs and elephants. The history of these figures is obscure. The best concentration is around the temple of Nandikeshwara at Mekke Kattu, near Udipi, where *bhootha* carved in the 1960s have replaced older ones now in museums. Jackwood *bhootha* figures are still carved to order by a family of the Gudigar caste in Uppunda, on the north Karnataka coast.

Scented sandalwood was traditionally only used for carving deities. The tree grows in the south, particularly in Karnataka where the craft is concentrated, but felling is now restricted, the timber rationed and dear. The carvers of the Ghat region of Karnataka are from the Gudigar community; the men generally work the wood in the compound while the women are indoors making wedding coronets and garlands from shola pith. Usually there is a sandalwood display piece in the house: Krishna driving Arjuna's chariot into battle is a common favourite.

There are some sandal-carvers in the north, in Jaipur, Ahmedabad, Delhi and Varanasi. In Churu (Rajasthan), Malchand Jangid, a carpenter by caste, used to make sandalwood almonds, even hinged in wood, which open to reveal a tiny deity. Ram Ratan Sharma, on the other hand, was not born to the craft but started carving cakes of cheap soap as a boy, until he discovered his grand-mother's

A stone-cutter crafting high-relief work in marble, Agra (top); and a woodcarver at work in Mysore (above).

cache of sandalwood. Now, with tools he makes himself, he creates intricate objects – lockets, flowering plants – full of hidden compartments that open to reveal gods, or village scenes.

Wooden toys remain popular in rural areas despite the onslaught of slicker plastic. At fairs rough little trucks and pairs of wheels that rotate a propeller when pushed are cheap and sell well. Still crude but attractive are the brightly painted buses, trucks and autorickshaws made in Trivandrum. There are more refined models, however; the little port of Beypore is noted for its teak sailing vessels, many of which are exported to the Persian Gulf, and with them go models, some more than 2 metres (6½ feet) in length. Children and adults alike used to collect around the puppeteer when he came to a village, but with the advent of film and television, most now seem to find stories enacted by mere puppets unsatisfying. They are still made, however, mostly in Bassi (Rajasthan) and coastal Karnataka, but they are often aimed at the souvenir market. Some dolls are still carved but many are lathe-turned to patterns not essentially Indian.

Chennapatna (Karnataka) is noted for its painted wooden goods ranging from large deities to dolls and realistic copies of animals, fruit and vegetables. Carpenters in Gokak and Kinhal, also in Karnataka, Sawantwadi (Maharashtra) and Nirmal (Andhra Pradesh) make similar toys. At Gokak they use light, soft *hariwal* wood, which is shaped with a 2-inch chisel, filed, then sandpapered. The surface is covered with a mixture of zinc oxide and glue, then painted. The mammals and birds made at Nirmal are especially good, assembled from roughly carved parts moulded together with a compound of tamarind seed and sawdust to form smooth, rounded forms. Nirmal was once famous for its painted wooden vessels – in particular a large covered platter – but demand has now faded. Often one craft has close associations with another. Not far from a textile centre, there will be a concentration of men specializing in carving printing-blocks, as can be seen at Sanganer (Rajasthan) and Pethapur (Gujarat). The block is generally a slice of *shisham* cut across the trunk, its surface planed and covered with a white paste. The paper design is pinned onto it and the shapes cut out with a miniature chisel or pierced with a bow-drill.

Woodcraft is threatened more by the inability of the government to control exploitation of depleted resources than by mass-production in alternative materials. The legislation exists, but forest officers are under pressure to ignore illegal lorry-loads of timber following backroads out of the Himalayan foothills or the rain forests of the Western Ghats. The dearer and rarer the timber, the more organized the illegal exploitation – the sandalwood smugglers of Karnataka form a prosperous little community. There are, of course, ambitious replanting projects but corruption renders them feeble. One state minister is known to have commented that had the local forestry accounts of funds drawn for tree-planting projects represented genuine action the whole desert state of Rajasthan should by that time have been covered in woodland. The rape of the softwood forests of Himachal Pradesh and Uttar Pradesh has received wide attention because of the destruction wrought on the environment, but the resulting reduced resources have caused timber prices to soar. As wood becomes dearer the craftsman is less able to compete with mass-produced versions of objects traditionally wooden. But even within the timber industry rapid mechanization is fast making the craftsman redundant.

A painted toy elephant, from Raghurajpur, Orissa.

15 RIGHT Pindli kuduku *(bride and groom dolls) carved out of raktchandan, a local hardwood, at Tiruchanar village, Andhra Pradesh. They are sold as temple souvenirs in Tirupati.*

16 LEFT *A jali-work window seen through two painted and moulded archways inside the City Palace at Jaipur.*

17 ABOVE *The work of roadside craftsmen in Varanasi, a carved stone statue of Dr Ambedkar, the champion of the outcastes at the time of Independence, awaits a customer.*

18 RIGHT *A 1760s stone figure of a frock-coated Dutchman guards the entrance to Rao Lakhaji's memorial chhatri in Bhuj, Kutch (Gujarat). Ram Singh Malam, the architect, spent eighteen years in Holland before returning to serve Lakhaji, the ruler of Kutch.*

19 ABOVE LEFT *Detail of a carved wooden lintel from north Bengal depicting a scene from the* Ramayana *in which Hanuman, the monkey chieftain, is worshipping Rama and Sita.*

20 LEFT *A carved and painted wooden toy horse from Jaipur, Rajasthan.*

21 ABOVE *A ceramic doorknob on a carved and painted wooden door to a village house in Kangra district, Himachal Pradesh.*

22 RIGHT *A* bhootha *figure, which is in the process of being shaped from jackwood by a family of Gudigar carvers at Uppunda, coastal Karnataka.*

23 ABOVE *Carved wooden brackets featuring female figures, from an old* patara *(chest), Saurashtra, Gujarat.*

24 ABOVE RIGHT *Miniature deities (Hanuman, left, and Krishna, right) used for personal worship by roadside vendors in Rajasthan.*

25 RIGHT *A carved wooden bracket from an old* patara *(left), and a freestanding* putli *(wooden doll), both from Saurashtra, Gujarat.*

26 ABOVE *A carved wooden doorway plaque,*
from Saurashtra, Gujarat.

27 RIGHT *A carved wooden pillar of Ganesh,*
the elephant-headed son of Shiva, from Tamil Nadu.

28, 30 A kavadh, *a prop for itinerant story-tellers, from the village of Bassi in south-east Rajasthan. As the story unfolds, the doors are opened to reveal scenes from Hindu mythology.* BELOW *The partially opened kavadh* displays panels depicting Vishnu being sheltered by the many-headed cobra, Ganesh the elephant-headed god, and Krishna playing his flute. Surya and Chandra, the sun and the moon in their chariots, appear at the top of the doors.

29 BELOW *A painted wood and cloth shrine to Jagannath, his brother Balabhadra and his sister Subhadra, made in Raghurajpur for sale in the nearby temple town of Puri, Orissa.*

31 A figure of the goddess Durga riding her tiger, made of painted wood and tamarind paste, from Kondapalli, Andhra Pradesh.

32 A painted, lathe-turned sindura from Varanasi, Uttar Pradesh. It holds the vermilion powder that the bridegroom applies to the parting in the bride's hair once the wedding ceremony has been completed.

49

33, 34 LEFT *A Shaivite figure on pilgrimage, and a figurine of Ganesh, the elephant-headed god. Both are made of painted and varnished wood and tamarind paste, in Cherial, Warangal district, Andhra Pradesh. Such figures are used as props in the day-long stories that are told to local pastoralists by the Mandhets, itinerant performers.*

35 ABOVE *A festival mask from Orissa. Such masks are made in Raghurajpur, Puri and in Koraput.*

36 RIGHT *A wooden head of Sita, wife of Rama, carved and painted for parading through the streets of Tamil Nadu at temple festivals.*

37 ABOVE LEFT *A carved wooden grain measure, from central India.*

38 ABOVE *Wooden sandals known as* khadaun, *worn by pious Hindus. Decorated with* tarkashi *(inlaid slivers of brass), in Mainpuri, Uttar Pradesh.*

39 LEFT *A nine-sided painted jackwood box known as a* naturapetty, *with ornate brass hinges and lock, from Kerala.*

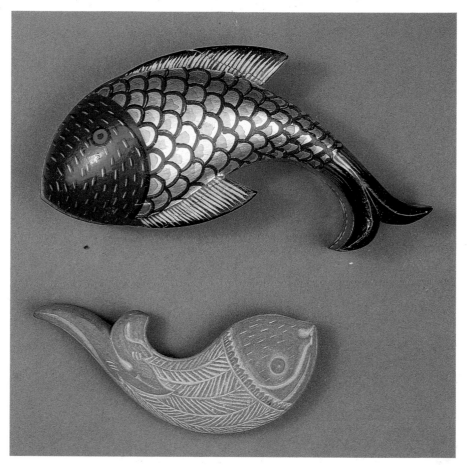

40, 41 ABOVE LEFT *Wooden architectural elements carved in the form of a horse and lion, from Saurashtra, Gujarat.*

42 BOTTOM LEFT *A carved sandalwood mirror-case from Shimoga district, Karnataka.*

43 ABOVE *A painted and varnished box shaped as a fish, from Nirmal, Andhra Pradesh (above), and a carved sandstone fish from Bikaner, Rajasthan.*

44, 45 *Carved sandstone elephants outside a mason's yard in Sikandra, Rajasthan, on the main highway between Agra and Jaipur.*

46 RIGHT *A black granite Ganesh, carved in Mamallapuram, Tamil Nadu. These images are sold by the roadside for household shrines.*

CHAPTER III

BRONZE, BRASS AND IRON

The inhabitants of India were early practitioners of metalwork. Excavations at the Indus Valley site of Mohenjo-Daro revealed a number of bronze objects and even a copper statuette of a dancing girl cast by the lost-wax process (see p. 62) which dates from c. 2000 BC. At contemporary Kalibangan (Rajasthan), archaeologists have unearthed copper beads, bangles and weapons. As in Mughal times, and still today, the Aravalli hills that cross Rajasthan were then a primary source of tin and copper ore. Much later, ironcraft, too, would offer its surprises – beside the Qutb Minar, the great towering minaret south of Delhi, stands a solid iron pillar 7.2 metres (23 1/2 feet) high bearing an inscription dating it to the 5th century AD. In Europe the forging of such a massive piece of iron would only have been possible comparatively recently. Zinc – with copper, the essential ingredient in brass manufacture – requires a particularly complex smelting process, only known to European metallurgists in the 1720s. Recent excavations at Zawar (southern Rajasthan) have revealed evidence of zinc smelting probably as far back as the 14th century.

Surrounding countries turned to India for fine metal-casting. There are 11th-century records of old copper and bronze vessels being exported through Aden to be recast in India, and it is probable that during the 16th and 17th centuries much Iranian metalware was actually made in the Punjab.

Until the 20th century, copper, brass and bell-metal ware was used in India as glass, china and silver ware was used in European households. Muslims tended to prefer copper and Hindus brass, although both chose silver for *piyali* (drinking vessels). Large numbers of artisans distributed widely through the country fed a huge demand for metalware. Copper vessels were usually beaten out from sheet metal, the noise of which was so ubiquitous that the British named a common, bright green bird 'the coppersmith' because of its monotonous 'tonk, tonk, tonk...' call. The form of some commonly used vessels has changed little from Buddhist times. *Lotas,* which are small rimmed pots, and large water pots very similar to those excavated or depicted in sculpture and murals of the early centuries AD are still being produced.

Nasik (Maharashtra), one of Hinduism's holiest cities, was in the late 19th century a major centre of copper- and brass-beating as well as of various forms of casting. The craftsmen, Kansara by caste (*kansa* means 'brass'), were concentrated in Tambat Lane (*tamba* means 'copper'). There the craft survives as a government-supported co-operative comprising a few old men of five Hindu households who tell how, as recently as 1970, a walk along the lane was a deafening experience. Today they no longer beat out the complete water pot (their staple product).

47 LEFT *A bronze portrayal of Nataraja, Shiva as Lord of the Dance, surrounded by a nimbus of flames, cast in Tamil Nadu.*

Instead, they buy in the bottom (most taxing) section machine-pressed, and only hammer it for decoration after brazing the parts together. A basic requirement of the coppersmith is a solid, hollowed-out work surface on which to beat his vessels into shape. In Nasik the men use massive pieces of defunct machinery, cogs with their shafts removed.

At Belgaum (Karnataka) thirty-four families, all Muslim, are employed in the suburb of Shahpur, where they carry out the complete process. Here, the work surfaces are great rounded boulders, kidney-shaped in section, with a deep hollow cut into the top, worn sculpturally smooth from years of use. Some of these anvil stones lie abandoned by the roadside, symbols of the contraction of the craft. To produce the lower section of a water pot, two men with large, heavy wooden mallets alternately beat a circular sheet of copper whilst a third manoeuvres the developing form on the stone anvil. Later, this is further shaped by a single worker using a smaller mallet. The upper section is similarly beaten out, then a central disc cut from it to accommodate the neck. The fringes of these two parts become frilly and pleated, as the copper sheet is deformed and stretched. These undulations are taken out with an iron hammer against an iron anvil. The neck itself is fashioned from a strip of copper which is bent, then brazed into a tube, its rim being either a flange hammered out from it, or else a strong ring of brass brazed on to the body of the pot.

The three sections are brazed together using a mixture of four parts brass to one of zinc. The sides of the pot are then beaten with an iron hammer against a specially shaped iron anvil. This is a bar bent up at right-angles at one end, so that it can be inserted into a vessel and applied to its inner wall, counterposing the hammer blows. This produces the characteristic dimpled pattern of hammered metalwork. Although the lower section is ready-pressed, the Nasik men expect to complete only two pots a day, little different from those of Belgaum where an old man reckoned a pot to be four hours' labour. With many people still purchasing new copper vessels as water-carriers and standard dowry items, the production centres of the south have the ethos of a living, if shrinking, craft.

Not all items hammered into shape are large, but in general the making of smaller objects is the province of a different community of craftsmen. Small bowls, cigarette boxes and *paan daan* (boxes made to contain the spices, leaves and tools associated with betel chewing) are still handmade in many parts of the country. In the old city of Hyderabad, in Andhra Pradesh, such work employs a few men in the street of Irani Gali, who beat the basic shape out of a brass sheet. It is then decorated with repoussé designs and finally plated with silver or German silver (an alloy quite devoid of silver itself).

Brass, as currently defined, is an alloy of two parts copper to one of zinc; in the past, the proportions were variable. Uttar Pradesh has long been the most significant state in the production of brassware, where the city of Moradabad has now superseded Varanasi as the centre of this craft. Here most metal-working and decorating techniques are practised. The narrow streets are busy with donkey carts, cycle rickshaws and men with head-baskets carrying bright utensils, whole or in parts, from one household to another where the next process in the sequence of production will be completed. The craftsmen, almost entirely Muslim, describe the usual alloy as being made up of half copper, a quarter zinc and the remainder waste brass from a multitude of sources, including old vehicle radiators.

A design depicting an elephant with birds, engraved on a brass pot from Jaipur, Rajasthan.

The repoussé worker is another artisan in the chain of production: plain, completed articles arrive at his shop for decoration. Pots and bowls are filled with a molten mixture of lacquer or resin, brickdust and oil, then put into cold water so that it sets. This supports the thin metal sheet while the pattern is beaten into it. When the design is completed, the vessels are inverted on a frame and heated with a blow-lamp so that the mixture melts and flows out, ready to be used again. Much of the repoussé work is done on a flat surface, in which instance large pieces of some intricacy are laid on a wooden bed.

Most of the brass articles are sand-cast. An occasional sight in many parts of India is the itinerant caster of images. He arrives in a small town and sets up his pitch with a little charcoal fire and a crucible full of brass waste – old screws, bits of pipe, parts of Tilley lamps – whilst his wife or child operates a bellows. He has a selection of images of popular deities for his clients to choose from, but will reproduce their own favourite figure if it is small enough to fit in his casting box. The sand must be fine and slightly damp, so that it takes and holds a detailed imprint. He beats down the sand then places the image face down in it and closes the box. Carefully re-opening it, he removes the figure without disturbing the sand. The molten metal is poured in through a channel in the side of the box and a bright new image is turned out onto the ground to the pleasure of the surrounding crowd, for whom this is no small entertainment.

In the cities of Uttar Pradesh, sand-casting, still a small-scale industry, is far more geared to mass production. Units of three or four teams of men regularly manufacture a large number of identical pieces, often cast in several sections. A team usually consists of three: a boy to operate the bellows and two men to fill the casting boxes and pour the molten metal. The furnace is set beneath the floor, opening as a round chimney down which the crucible is lowered. It is fuelled with small fragments of coke, which fill the air with noxious fumes.

A small brass vase may be cast in four parts – the neck, the centre as two hemispheres, and the base – if possible, more than one section being cast at the same time. The boxes are either cylindrical for large items or rectangular. A man sits setting out little inverted egg-cup-shaped pieces on a metal sheet and within a rectangular frame. These are a single section of a small vase. He then pours a mixture of damp sand and ash around and over the pieces to be copied and beats it firmly so that only the bottom tips of the pieces project above the surface. Clean white sand is then spread over the surface. The next rectangular section of the box is fitted above the first and an equal number of pieces of the next section of the vessel set out, each vase touching the projecting part of one of the lower group. The same sand mixture is poured in and around these and duly beaten down. Into the sand within each little cup a slip of metal called a *makora* is pressed, its function being to increase the pressure on the sand within the cup and act as a core for the sand structure. A white powder, *suhaga* (borax) is spattered over the surface and a final layer of sand added over it.

Now comes the most difficult process: the box must be opened gently and each brass object removed without disturbing its sand cast. It is then inverted and the other layer of pieces removed. The box is closed with care and tilted so that the 'spout' of the bottom section becomes a slot in the upper part of the top. Into this the molten metal is poured, channels in the sand allowing it to flow easily into each mould. It sets immediately, the box is opened and the contents tipped out; the sand

A Muslim metal-worker decorating a thin-walled brass pot with repoussé work, in Moradabad, Uttar Pradesh, India's major brass-working centre.

will be damped and re-used. The new brass sections are put to one side, destined to be brazed together at another unit. Faulty pieces are returned to the crucible for the next casting. From timing the work at one unit, it was discovered that the whole process, from laying out the first pieces to emptying the box of its finished product, took about eight minutes. As soon as one batch is completed, the next begins.

There is a great diversity of objects cast, including small models of motorcycles with a circular space at the centre in which to fit a clock! Another line – sand-cast knuckle dusters – is produced at Aligarh (Uttar Pradesh), whilst nearby Hathras specializes in forgeries of ancient brass and bronze items for the antique market.

One popular form of embellishment is the painting of incised designs with coloured lacquer. The craftsman sits behind a small, raised fireplace burning charcoal, occasionally turning the handle which operates the bellows. At his side lies an assortment of sticks of lacquer, each a different colour. He heats a vessel, rotating it against a wooden cone over the red coals before applying the appropriate colour to the cut patterns. These colours overflow the borders of the carved-out shapes, but because these are recessed he can easily clean off the surplus by running a special bladed tool over the still-warm surface. The end result is gaudy, but popular on vases, *surahi* (flasks) and ornamental jugs for the home market.

Although hand-casting of brass is still widespread, many of the household utensils that keep the industry flourishing are now produced in other media or are made more cheaply on the conveyor belt. *Sarota* are a cross between scissors and nutcrackers, being both bladed and hinged. They are used to shave off slivers from the areca nut, destined to be mixed with spices and wrapped in betel leaf to make the popular stimulant, *paan*. The *sarota* was often shaped humorously as an animal or person, the handles being legs, arms or wings. The brass version disappeared with the advent of good steel. *Sarota* are made in Kutch (Gujarat), especially at Anjar and the nearby village of Rehat Kotara, but they are rarely decorated with anything more than incised floralwork. Kutch is also noted for its swords, spears, axe heads and handmade cutlery, particularly pen-knives with brass or horn handles. More vicious are the knives of Rampur (northern Uttar Pradesh) which often have fish-shaped handles cast in brass. Many of these are long-bladed flick knives, and Rampura knives frequently find mention in reports of murder or riot.

Locksmiths still practise their craft, but there can be little interest in handmade brass padlocks when far stronger steel versions are being mass-produced. The old ones were sometimes vast and extremely ingenious, with keys screwing in or pulling out as well as turning to release the catch. They still appear amongst the rusty metalware beside a bazaar locksmith, whose main function today is to replace lost keys or pick the locks.

The principle of sand-casting is integral to the manufacture of *bidri*-ware, a metalcraft unique to India. The name *bidri* derives from Bidar (Karnataka), a town that was once the capital of a sizeable Muslim-ruled state. Local tradition holds that during the 15th century the local ruler summoned some metalworkers from Persia to fulfil a contract. Once their task was finished, however, they settled in the town and developed a new technique of inlaying intricate brass and silver designs into a darkened zinc surface. Interestingly, this is thought to coincide with the development of zinc-smelting in Rajasthan.

A Muslim metal-worker adding the final touches to an engraved and lacquered brass tray, in Jaipur, Rajasthan.

The earliest surviving examples of *bidri* craftwork are 17th-century pieces, and *bidri*-ware, usually hookahs, bowls and vases, is also illustrated in miniatures of that period. By the 19th century the craft was dying out, but it was given a new lease of life, even expanded, thanks to the craft and industry exhibitions in the second half of the century, which brought it to wide public attention. Important *bidri* centres of that period such as Purnea and Murshidabad (West Bengal) and Lucknow have long dwindled to nothing, but *bidri*-ware is still produced in quantity in Bidar and Hyderabad.

A bidri-ware bowl with a silver inlay, made in Bidar in the 19th century.

The *bidri* craftsmen cast their own pieces, making a moulding 'clay' from sand, resin and oil (in proportions of 20:2:1), and apply borax to the 'clay' surface to prevent the metal sticking. Flasks, jugs or vases are usually cast in two sections, divided along the vertical axis. The alloy, variously described as nine to sixteen parts zinc to one of copper, is melted and poured into the casting box. If the vessel is being made in sections, it is soldered together before the whole surface is filed over and copper sulphate applied. This temporarily darkens the surface, contrasting sharply with the incised design and thus making the craftman's job easier. If he is sufficiently skilled he will sketch the motif freehand from memory, but more often he will rely on some form of *naqsha* ('map').

Once the outline is drawn, the engraver, fixing the piece in a vice, cuts out the pattern with a tiny hammer and chisel. Depending on the design, the inlaid pattern will either be formed from wire, which is cut to fill the incised grooves and forced into place with a blunt chisel-like tool, or from a silver sheet, which is laid over the design and beaten with the wooden end of a hammer so that the relief shows through. The outline is then cut out and the surplus silver removed.

After the silver has been inlaid the surface is filed over and buffed before being placed in a boiling mixture described by the craftsmen as ammonium chloride mixed with a special mud – some mention the addition of salt, saltpetre and copper sulphate to the brew. It is taken out after about ten minutes, the excess mud and salts washed off and oil applied. The surface cannot be buffed with anything abrasive since that would result in a lightening of the finish and so lessen the contrast. Today, commercial silver polish is used to bring out the inlay. The general output consists of vases, jugs, dishes, bowls, plates, ash trays, cigarette cases and even items as small as cufflinks.

Sarota, from Jodhpur, Rajasthan.

At many metalworking centres in India, including Moradabad, Bidar and Hyderabad, a relatively new and gloriously hideous development is the latest generation of aluminium casting. Dancers and deities cast in white aluminium have given way to what are called 'black metal' figures. These are cast in sections in mass-produced moulds, assembled and plated with copper oxide. The repertoire includes eagles, lions, 16th-century Europeans in ornate armour and even galleons. The *bidri* craftsmen remark that the local middle class far prefer these items to traditional *bidri*-ware.

Lost-wax casting, practised in ancient Egypt, was familiar to the Indus Valley civilization. The metal most commonly associated with this form of casting in recent times is 'bell metal', an alloy of four parts copper to one of tin. There are still a few active centres in Madhya Pradesh (where the tribal work of Bastar is particularly interesting), southern Uttar Pradesh, Bengal, Orissa and the southern states. The artisans of north and central India usually belong to the Kansari community.

In Kerala there are centres of lost-wax casting at Kasaragod, Trivandrum and Iranjalkuda, near Trichur. At Iranjalkuda, a busy co-operative casts both large and small objects in brass and bell metal. Certain ritual pieces such as the tall, tiered oil-lamp candelabra so widely used in southern temples, once exclusively made in bell metal, are now cast in brass. Some large vessels, including the flat, traditional *urale* used for cooking sweets for large communal meals given either at temples or by the wealthy, were almost always of bell metal, although they are now sometimes cast in aluminium.

To cast a *urale*, the worker first creates a solid core of clay mixed with mud, shaping it on a lathe to reproduce the form of the interior. This is dried and put back on the lathe, then, as it slowly rotates, hot wax is dripped onto the surface until its thickness is equal to that required in the finished item. This calls for a practised eye. The surface is then smoothed and some basic decoration added – perhaps a couple of lines around the circumference. Over the wax, a thin layer of fine liquid clay is applied and allowed to dry before a coarser clay mixed with the ground remnants of old moulds is coated over it. The thickness of this second layer varies with the size of the object, but 3 centimetres is usual for a medium-sized *urale*. Two openings are left in the casing, one on the upper rim and the other in the centre of the bottom of the finished vessel. The completed mould is allowed to dry in the sun before it is leant against a furnace fired with wood and coconut shells, with the rim hole at the bottom. The wax melts and drains out, and is collected in a bowl for re-use. Until recently, only beeswax was used, but this is now often replaced by commercially produced substitutes.

Casting takes place in the evening, allowing time for the furnace to reach optimum temperature (some 800°C). Both the moulds and the crucibles of metal are placed in the furnace, since heating the mould evacuates most of the air and encourages the molten metal to flow easily. The mould is then laid upside down and tilted so that the rim hole is uppermost. The metal is poured through the hole and as it fills the cavity left by the wax it forces any remaining air out through the rim hole. When the mould is full, the hole is blocked. Usually it is left overnight before the casing is broken to reveal the new piece. Some traditional bowls known as *warpu* have side handles that are cast separately and brazed on afterwards. The finished surface will be uneven and rough, needing chiselling over before being burnished in a lathe.

Amongst the many items manufactured in the Kerala workshops are the *urale* made for temple use, which measure up to one metre in diameter and weigh about 100 kg (220 lbs), large church bells for the significant Christian population of the state, and temple lamps that are cast in tiers, each with a shaft that screws into the tier below, and the whole crowned by a bird form.

Special variants of the craft are also produced. At Kollum in north Kerala there is a fading hookah manufacturing industry. Its output, aimed at the Middle East, has declined sharply since the Gulf War of 1991. The water bowl is made from a coconut shell filed so that its almost black inner layer is exposed, holes being cut in it to accommodate the pipes leading to the burning tobacco and to the mouthpiece. This shell is held between two finely decorated sections joined by sixteen strands of brass riveted across the nut's surface. The lost-wax technique used in its manufacture is here more complicated. The craftsman, generally of the blacksmith caste, builds up the basic wax form on a wooden last. He has his own handmade

A metal-worker in Kerala, filing down a urale *freshly cast by the lost-wax technique.*

arc-shaped lead moulds to produce the bands of decoration that run around the brasswork of the pipe. The decorative motifs are generally floral but sometimes include birds or fish. Each design is made in four or five sections then applied to the last, the curved shape reducing distortion when the design is fitted onto the round surface. The entire wax form is carefully fused together with a heated metal rod.

When the form is completed the whole translucent wax shell is lifted off the last and dipped into fine liquid clay, which forms a coat over it. After this has dried, it is covered with a coarser clay, which, too, is allowed to dry. The wax is drained from the mould and a crucible of metal, ten parts copper to seven of zinc, is actually built onto the top of the mould. The whole thing is put into the furnace with the crucible at the bottom, until a blue flame appears from a hole at the joint between the crucible and the mould. Then the complete mould is very gently tilted so that the metal flows into it.

Once a large industry through much of the country, the production of bronze mirrors is now confined to two families in Aranmula, in southern Kerala, and stands as yet another example of a craft product that has been outmoded by a mass-produced one. The process is a closely guarded secret, but it seems that the reflective surface is made of an alloy richer in tin than the surrounding frame and that this responds well to burnishing.

The most impressive lost-wax work is figurative, feeding a constant demand for portrayals of the godhead. Although the craft was once more widespread, it has largely faded from the north. It was in the south, during the Chola period, that Tamil craftsmen cast some of the finest of the world's figurative bronzes. The simple elegance and relaxed air of the deities coupled with their restrained decoration set them apart from any other South Asian bronze sculpture.

Tradition stipulates that metal images for worship in a temple should be cast either in *ashtadhata*, a sacred alloy of eight metals (gold, silver, copper, zinc, lead, tin, iron and mercury) or *panchaloha* (copper, brass, lead, silver and gold). In neither case is the proportion laid down, so, naturally, the costly ingredients are added only as a trace to satisfy the stipulations. In the north figurative work takes place in Varanasi and Srinagar near Mahoba (Uttar Pradesh), in the Bastar region of Madhya Pradesh and in several parts of West Bengal and Orissa, but generally only on small figures. There are several centres in the south, of which Swamimalai, near Thanjavur (Tamil Nadu) is the most important. There, many of the idols are destined for export to expatriate Hindu communities. The largest idol ever cast (almost 2.5 metres high and weighing 2600 kg), was made there, for a temple in Malaysia.

The makers of metal idols in southern India belong to the Sthapathy community. They create each figure in a number of different sections, each shaped by hand in an equal mixture of wax and *kungli*, a resinous substance imported from Kerala. The sections are assembled, smoothed over, then covered with fine liquid clay which, once dry, is coated with 2 to 3 centimetres of river mud. This is dried for a day before a final layer of mixture three parts clay to one of fine sand is applied some 7 to 8 centimetres thick. This last coat may be reinforced with iron rods before it is left to dry. Two apertures are left in the base of the mould.

The mould is lowered into a cow-dung fire, and tilted at such an angle that the wax, as it melts, drains out of one of the openings. The *panchaloha* alloy generally favoured consists of some 83 per cent copper, 15 per cent brass, 2 per cent lead and

A bronze statue of male and female Gond figures either side of a peepal tree.

traces of gold and silver. This is heated to 800 to 1000°C in a charcoal-fired pit furnace, poured into one of the apertures in the hot mould and left for a day to cool. Traditionally the head is revealed first. The image will invariably have a rough, uneven surface which must be filed smooth and sanded before the details of jewelry and clothing are incised. The facial features are always smoothed and engraved last, before the completed figure is burnished.

In Bastar, Madhya Pradesh, the traditional method of casting is another variation of the lost-wax process. The figures are generally small, depicting major or merely local deities, and apart from the head and arms they are hollow, built up on a core. This is made of a mixture of clay and sand covered with fine clay so that details can be clearly formed. When the figure is completed beeswax is squeezed through a syringe, producing a thread of wax to be wound around the figure until it is completely covered. The wax is then smoothed over. On this smooth surface the craftsman shapes the clothing, decoration and jewelry using more threads of wax, and it is these that give the characteristic appearance of Bastar figures. The technique known as *dokla* that is used by the tribals of Bengal and Orissa is rather similar.

In north India ironcraft is the province of the Lohar folk, both Hindu and Muslim. Some are itinerant tinkers whose encampments are a common and striking sight. They live beneath and around their unique, old-style carts, which are panelled with patterned ironwork. Although nomadic, all look to some town or village as the home of their community. Amongst the Muslim tribes are the Multani, from Multan, now in Pakistan, and the Nagauri, from Nagaur in Rajasthan. The most romantic tale is that of the Hindu Lohars from Chittor. According to this story, these people were swordsmiths to the Rana of Mewar, whose capital was in that great fort. When it was sacked by Akbar in the 16th century they took to the road, vowing never to settle until the Rana was again housed in Chittor. The Rana, however, founded a new capital – Udaipur – so that day never came and they continue to wander, returning to Chittor only for annual festivals.

Lohars beat iron into various agricultural implements and repair damaged goods. The whole family are involved in the craft, the women often doing the hardest work, wielding the heavy hammers whilst the men manoeuvre the iron on the anvil. It is widely thought inauspicious to do anything concerning iron, even to purchase iron items, on Saturdays.

Of all Indian crafts, those using base metals have been most affected by India's post-Independence industrialization. Tedious, labour-intensive methods of casting or beating metal into the required shapes can now be easily reproduced in factory conditions by mass-casting or machine-pressing. In most households the old utensils, cooking and water vessels are handmade of brass or iron, heavy, solid and made to last; some came into the house in the dowry of the grandmother. The newer items are machine-made in stainless steel or aluminium. It is difficult for craftsmen, even under the intensive organization that exists in Moradabad, to undercut factory prices. They can, however, more quickly turn themselves to producing a new form – sandcasting requires only the model. Metalcraft is in retreat. Only the itinerant repairers of brass pots, or the Lohars who attract repairs or one-off creations from the neighbourhood in which they have camped, continue to thrive.

48 RIGHT *A brass Shiva lingam bearing the face of the deity, cast in three pieces in the Deccan, probably near Poona. It is shaded by the seven-headed cobra.*

49 ABOVE *Cast brass figurines of the deity Khandoba, which
adorn the base of large wooden poles carried in procession at
festivals in southern Maharashtra.*

50–2 OPPOSITE *A brass cigarette box from Bombay, in
the form of a 1940s American limousine* (TOP); *a candlestick
mounted on a brass bull, from central India* (LEFT); *and
a brass box with its lid fashioned in the shape of a woman's
head, from Dinajpur, north Bengal.*

53 LEFT *A shrine to a Jain* tirthankar *(who is surrounded by his attendants), made of bronze with silver details, from Rajasthan.*

54 ABOVE *A copper storage pot for valuables, known as a* dabalo, *from the Saurashtra peninsula, Gujarat. It is often buried for safekeeping.*

55 RIGHT *A bronze equestrian figure of Khandoba, from Bastar.*

56 LEFT *Brass water pots from Indore, Madhya Pradesh. They are designed to be carried back from the well balanced on a woman's head – the smaller upper pot fits snugly on top of the lower one.*

57 ABOVE *This jewelry box from Hyderabad, Andhra Pradesh, has been decorated with a floral pattern using the* bidri *technique. By this process, the pattern is etched into the zinc base and then painstakingly inlayed with silver.*

58 RIGHT *A 19th-century* bidri-*ware vase inlaid with floral designs, probably from Purnea, West Bengal.*

CHAPTER IV

JEWELRY, GOLD AND SILVER

Rarely in the world has jewelry formed such an important part of personal adornment as it has in India. Archaeological evidence illustrating this dates back to the famous dancing girl of Harappa, an angular but alluring figurine naked but for body jewelry and bangles on one arm stretching from the wrist almost to her shoulder. Sculpture from the Gandhara and Gupta periods again shows a minimum of clothing but an abundance of jewelry. Ornaments adorn hair, neck, ears, wrists, arms and ankles, waist and toes.

The instinct for self-adornment is manifest very early on in the development of mankind, motivated not only by the urge to decorate and beautify, but also by the need for personal talismans to provide protection against potentially destructive forces. At first, shells, pebbles, seeds and other small natural objects were used; indeed, seeds and wooden beads are still worn by holy men as sign of their religious affiliation. Shaivites wear *rudraksha* beads, which are large, round, deeply sulcated seeds, and Vaishnavites wear necklaces of *tulsi* seeds or sandalwood. After the development of metal-working, however, gold and silver – durable, gleaming and brilliant – grew to be treasured and used for all manner of adornment. Gold and silver were coveted not only for their intrinsic beauty but also their relative scarcity, and they became highly valuable.

The practice of setting gemstones into precious metal probably originated in the Middle East, but India, with its wealth of precious and semi-precious stones and its many trade links, has a long history of gem-set jewelry. India also had an abundance of ivory from its great herds of elephants, and one of the most important pearl beds off Tuticorin, in the Palk Straits between south India and Sri Lanka. With mines for gold and silver, rubies, garnets, agate, diamonds, tigers' eyes and the riches generated from local agriculture and the trade in local cloth and handicrafts, Indians of some means had many different types of jeweled ornamentation available to them.

Jewelry has always functioned as a material repository of wealth, and its role as such was prevalent all through the social scale. The rulers of Indian states, permanently threatened by dynastic upheavals and internecine feuding, needed to hold their wealth in a form that was extremely compact and portable and could be easily hidden or traded. Costly jewelry satisfied these conditions ideally, and there are many stories of Indian princes fleeing into the desert night with their gold, jewels and pearls, buying security from foreign rulers and sometimes even the military help needed to regain their kingdoms.

The merchants of India were subject to the same uncertain political climate, and therefore also hoarded their wealth in the form of jewelry. Indeed they

59 LEFT *A tray displaying the wares of a Jaipur jeweler's shop. Antique silver boxes and a statuette are seen beside enamelled and turquoise set containers, earrings, pendants and bangles.*

employed a special caste of 'gem-carriers', whose job was to transport jewelry secretly and safely across the length and breadth of India. Even amongst the poorer classes, jewelry was always valued much more for the intrinsic worth of its metal (usually silver) than for its workmanship, as this could be redeemed in times of drought, famine or war. Even today a woman of peasant or pastoralist caste in India will be weighed down by heavy silver jewelry which she will never take off. She is the family's walking treasury, its wealth secure from all but the most daring and brutal thieves. Up until this century a Hindu woman's personal jewelry was her only legal property; a baby girl will be given her first ornament at birth.

The jewelry of the rich and the poor could traditionally be differentiated by the metal from which it was made: the ruling elite, the merchants and priests wore gold while the lower castes (Sudras, untouchables and tribals) were confined to silver and sometimes even base metal. This distinction still prevails today, although anyone with any pretension to wealth will buy gold if they can. Another distinction can be made between urban and village jewelers. The village jeweler's art is confined to the making of crudely fashioned but heavy silver ornaments which have to be bent on and off with the help of the village blacksmith. The village jeweler works metal much in the fashion of the blacksmith – forging, casting, beating, then decorating by simple engraving. A city jeweler, however, will also work with gold and gems, and create filigree and repoussé jewelry; he can also granulate, emboss, chase and engrave in a much more sophisticated manner than his village counterpart. Beautiful enamelling achieved an astounding level of excellence in Mughal times and is still practised today in Jaipur, Nathdwara, Varanasi and Calcutta.

Precious and semi-precious stones feature abundantly in Indian jewelry and come from a wide variety of sources: lapis lazuli from Afghanistan, turquoise from Iran, the United States and Tibet (although a synthetic substitute is now manufactured in India), rubies from Orissa and Burma, garnets from Orissa and Bihar, emeralds from the Panna mines in Madhya Pradesh (where diamonds are also mined) and from Brazil. Sri Lanka and Burma supply sapphires, and stones of a very high quality are found in Kashmir. Agate beads are still cut at Khambhat in Gujarat, as they have been since ancient times.

Diamond-cutting is centred on Surat, and to a lesser extent Bombay and Rajkot. Most diamonds are now imported from Africa, although until 1725 India was the world's only source; such legendary stones as the 'Kohinoor' ('Mountain of Light') came from India. Precious stones are polished in many cities throughout India, but Jaipur is by far the most important. To achieve the desired angles and finish, the polisher sets the stone on the end of a specially carved stick and holds it against either a bow-driven or electrically powered grindstone.

One of the marks of the genius of Indian jewelry is the way in which small pieces of gemstone – often no more than flakes – are embedded in the surrounding metal. This is known as a *kundan* setting (the clasp setting of gems was a Western innovation only introduced into India in the late 19th century). These flakes have no intrinsic value, yet with the aid of various contrivances such as mirrors set in lacquer placed beneath them, they are made to glitter and sparkle in a unique way.

Whatever his range of skill and materials, the jeweler's tools are still very simple: hammers, an anvil, mandrel, punches and gravers, tongs, clamps and fine tweezers, and a J-shaped blow-pipe for soldering and annealing the metal. A cubic

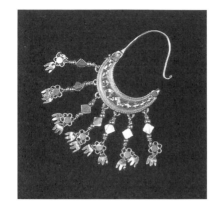

A pair of finely worked gold earrings from northern India.

doming-block inset with a multiplicity of different shapes, on which different sections of jewelry are beaten out, is essential to the craft, as are shears to cut metal sheets and a draw-plate for drawing through wire of different gauges. Surrounded by all these tools and his charcoal brazier, the craftsman will squat to work, in a rather cramped workplace that is usually raised off the ground to about waist-level.

Most jewelry is commissioned. The jeweler charges for the weight of the metal and other materials, as well as a fee for working it. Often as fashions and economic circumstances change over the years, an old piece is taken to a jeweler to be reworked. It may be melted down and totally reworked, or perhaps a large, rather cumbersome piece will be broken up and turned into several different ornaments.

In India, a jeweler is traditionally regarded with much suspicion: it is always assumed that he will cheat you if he gets a chance, and this reputation has even given rise to various sayings ('If a piece of jewelry goes to a jeweler nine times, there will be nothing left'!). The village jeweler rarely profits greatly from his trade, however; nor do the city craftsmen, who usually specialize in one specific craft, such as casting, chasing or engraving. It is the big-city jeweler, with a busy retail trade and sometimes many craftsmen in his employ, who may generate enough surplus capital to act as a banker.

A silver and enamel talisman depicting the mother-goddess, from the Kulu valley, Himachal Pradesh.

Indian jewelry-making was probably at its height at the time of the Mughal empire, when new-found political stability and consequent economic prosperity combined with the cosmopolitan nature of the Mughal ruling class (who attracted craftsmen from all over the Muslim world) produced jewelry and other craftwork of an incredibly high standard. Under the Mughal system of honours and patronage, position, income and wealth were only granted for life and reverted back to the emperor at death – very little was to be inherited by a nobleman's heirs. This inevitably led to ostentatious consumption. The royal Mughals themselves set up *kharkhanas* (court workshops) for all manner of crafts and attracted artisans from Persia and other centres of excellence.

At the breakup of the Mughal empire in the 18th century and the dissolution of the court workshops, jewelers and other craftsmen migrated to the courts of Rajasthan and other princely states, and to the courts of localized Muslim powers such as that of Oudh. There they continued their work in the old Mughal style for their new patrons. Jaipur state had had the closest relations with the Mughals, and was also relatively close to Delhi and Agra, the Mughal capitals. Consequently Jaipur soon became a centre of craft excellence, especially in jewelry. Enamelling, a Mughal forte, was intended to protect gold, which in its pure state is soft and malleable and wears away over the course of time. The Mughal fashion was to set the obverse of the pieces with gems and pearls and to protect the reverse, which rubbed against the skin of the wearer, with enamelling, although since the 19th century, enamelling has no longer been restricted to the reverse of the piece.

The skill of enamelling was brought from Lahore to Jaipur by Hindu Punjabis who later adopted Sikhism. The process entails fixing or fusing differently coloured vitreous glazes onto the surface of the metal. Each colour of glaze fuses at a different temperature, and the art of the enameller lies in fusing these glazes in the right order, starting with white, which fuses at the highest temperature, down through to red, which fuses at the lowest temperature. The colours were once provided by families of bangle-makers in Lahore, but now come from Amritsar.

Once the enameller has added the glaze to the gouged-out channel, he inserts it into a charcoal-burning furnace made out of an old clay pot before proceeding one by one through the other colours without allowing them to mix into each other or permitting an already fused glaze to melt. As with so much Indian craftsmanship, temperatures and measures are gauged with an experienced eye.

There are many different types of enamelling, and the variety traditionally practised in India is known as *champlevé*. *Champlevé* is the opposite of *cloisonné* enamelling, in which the surface of the object is built up with tiny walls to form the cells into which the enamel can be fused. With *champlevé*, the enameller gouges out channels or troughs in the surface of the metal and fills them with enamel. The ridges of the metal left between the channels form the outline of the design and help to keep the differently coloured areas of enamel from running into each other. The main centres for enamelling are Jaipur, Nathdwara, Varanasi – famous for its rosy hues – and Calcutta. There is a substitute for enamel called *thewa*, which is still made to a limited extent in Pratapgarh in southern Rajasthan. With this technique, a frame of silver wire is covered with gold leaf and set flush into a softened layer of green enamel or glass. Silver foil is placed behind the glass to enhance its brilliance.

Hindu and Muslim jewelry has always been quite different in style, but the Mughal fashions often amalgamated diverse Hindu and Muslim influences, and Mughal styles are still prevalent in northern India (in such popular items as anklets with bells on them and *jhumka* earrings with pendant bell shapes). Nose rings, whilst originally a Muslim fashion, are now found in both Muslim and Hindu communities all over India.

There are many jewelry-making centres specializing in a particular regional style. In northern India the best work is to be found in Jaipur, Kutch, Bikaner and Murshidabad. Centres that could once boast superlative craftsmanship, such as Bundi in Rajasthan, no longer produce fine work, although quality jewelry can be found in Hathras near Mathura in Uttar Pradesh, Deesa in north Gujarat, and in Rajkot (although here much of the production has been mechanized).

The jewelry of western India, where there is an abundance of silver and extensive trade relations with Arabia, the Persian Gulf, the Middle East and East Africa, shares similarities with the chunky silver jewelry of this essentially Arab and Muslim world. Although some of the work is figurative – the hero pendants of Rajasthan, for instance, and the *makara* (dragon) head endings on bangles – much of the design and embellishment of western Indian jewelry is essentially abstract and geometric, effects which are achieved through the building up of granulation and embossing.

Ivory bangles were once commonly worn in Rajasthan and Gujarat as a whole series of thin bracelets which covered the lower arm of unmarried girls and extended up the upper arm of married women. The bracelets increase in diameter, in accordance with the shape of both a woman's arm and an elephant's tusk. The ivory, once indigenous, has long been imported from Africa; much of it was coloured red with henna dye. Thankfully, since the banning of the ivory trade, most of these bangles have been replaced with plastic ones produced by local bangle-makers. In Gujarat, however, women of pastoral castes such as the Rabari will still wear a large section of elephant tusk on their left arms. (In north-east India the Naga traditionally use sections of local ivory as armlets.)

A silverwork hero pendant, from Rajasthan.

Ears of both men and women are pierced in many places, through the lobe, along the outer rim and through the middle cartilage. A solid twisted, spring-like torque of silver or sometimes base metal, known as a *hasli*, is worn as a necklace by peasant and pastoral women. Children at the toddler stage, before they start to wear many clothes, wear a pubic ornament in the shape of a *bo* leaf which hangs from a silver chain around their waists. Waist chains are also commonly worn by women and are believed to control the size of the waist.

The jewelers of Himachal Pradesh, centred around the Rajput hill princedoms of Kangra, Chamba, Mandi and Kulu, were famous for their technical expertise and mastery of the enamelling process – their work is characterized by a predominance of deep blues and greens. Working mainly in silver, the craftsmen created elliptical fretwork anklets containing jangling balls, solid lion-headed bangles and exquisite enamelled semi-spherical hair ornaments, an enamelled peepal-leaf-shaped forehead ornament, a marriage necklace known as a *chandrahaar* made of enamelled plaques and silver chains, and enamelled pendants with vivid descriptions of the mother goddess, which look almost Nordic in their design. The jewelers who cater for the inhabitants of the isolated mountain district of Kinnaur create some of the most dramatic pieces. With the exception of the jewelers of Mandi and Kulu, however, who still create mother-goddess heads of a stark and simple beauty from thin sheet gold, the quality of workmanship has declined.

Ladakhi women wear a head ornament known as a *perak*, which runs from the forehead over the head and down the back. The *perak* incorporates all the woman's wealth, including rough, uncut lumps of raw turquoise and coral which are set in silver and attached to a red ground cloth. The weight of the piece is partially borne by two sheepskin ear-flaps sewn to the backing cloth which are tied into the woman's hair.

In Kashmir, parts of West Bengal and Cuttack in Orissa, filigree silver is the speciality; filigree necklaces are also popular in Lucknow and Kanpur in Uttar Pradesh. In the Mohammadiya Bazar and Mansik Patna areas of Cuttack, silver comes in biscuit form from Bombay. It is melted in a crucible and poured into moulds the size of pencils. When it is set, it is drawn out into wire by machine, decreasing from the thickest gauge on the machine to the thinnest. The wire is annealed by making it red hot and then cooling it down. It is then pulled by hand through a draw-plate until it is of the requisite thinness, when it can be built up into nose rings and earrings, pendants and freestanding ornaments such as models of ships or perhaps the Taj Mahal. In Cuttack, filigree is commonly known as *tarkashi*.

Calcutta and the other jewelry-making centres in West Bengal produce the elephant bangle, a symbol of married status among Bengali women. Usually made of gold wrapped around a core of iron, they are embellished with a circle of elephant heads (the traditional way of warding off the evil eye from the husband). Women remove these bangles when their husband dies. Poorer Bengali women wear a single conch-shell bangle on each wrist, accompanied by one or two red glass bangles, and these also indicate married status. The conches that come from Kutch and south India are cut by machine in Calcutta, Bishnupur and other centres, and these then have floral and vegetal designs carved or filed on them.

South Indian jewelry differs quite markedly from that of the north. Its designs are taken from nature, with flowers, lotus buds, grass stalks and even *rudraksha*

A Ladakhi woman wearing a perak *headdress of uncut turquoise and coral, which is attached with sheepskin earflaps.*

beads imitated in gold or silver. Gems are used for their symbolism as much as for their decorative effect. (Jewels always had a symbolic significance. In many parts of India the wearing of the *nau ratan* – the nine gems – was seen as both talismanic and astrologically auspicious. Astrologers and faith healers prescribe the wearing of personally auspicious stones in such a way that they are always in contact with the skin.)

The important jewelry-making centres of the south are Hyderabad, Bangalore, Mysore, Ootacamund and Thanjavur. Hyderabad is a major centre for drilling and dealing in cultured pearls. Kolhapur in Maharashtra is famous for its gold jewelry, and is the original home of the snake chains which are now mainly mass-produced in Hyderabad. The ornaments of Tamil Nadu, southern Karnataka and Andhra Pradesh have many similarities. Although there are individual pieces unique to each region, others like the *odiyaanam* (gold waist belt), *vanki* (armlet) and *jimikki* (eardrop) are common to all parts of south India. Prominent among items of personal adornment here is the *paambadam* worn by rural Tamil women. *Paambadam* are great lumps of gold; although they are in fact all one piece they represent six earrings, and are so heavy that they pull the ear lobes down to shoulder level. Rural Tamil men wear ear-studs of single stones called *kadukkan*, while the normal ear ornaments of the women are lotus-shaped ear-studs of rubies and diamonds, called *kammal*. Below this hangs the *jimikki*, a bell-shaped eardrop, either in gold or stone-studded. Sometimes another eardrop, a *lolaakku*, is worn, which can be of any design, although usually this has a floral motif. There is little enamelwork in the region, although Hyderabad was historically an important centre for this kind of work.

The culture of Kerala is markedly different in many ways to that of the south, and produces jewelry with certain unique qualities; floral and bird forms are exaggerated, sometimes to a fantastic extent. As in the rest of India, most communities have a clearly identifiable but limited vocabulary of jewelry pieces. The prosperous Moplah Muslim group, for instance, wear the *kashmalla* (a necklace of gold sovereigns), the *kannadi vala* (a bangle comprised of many polished surfaces), and the *gala mini* (a tight choker); all of these are crafted specifically for them by the local Hindu jewelers.

One of the best places to see the most splendid jewelry, both worn and in the making, is Kutch. In the backstreets of the city of Bhuj is the jewelry bazaar. The first few shops have gained smart new glass fronts and exhibit glittering trays of silver and gold rings, bangles and nose rings, with a few old pieces in the window to give extra colour. Further into the bazaar are the smaller, old-fashioned shops with just a bench or cushion for customers, and a glass case on a very low table in which they display their more limited selection.

Interspersed among these smaller shops are the workshops, where artisans of all ages ply the traditional tools of their trade – blow-pipes, alongside the now ever-present blow-torches and electric grinding and polishing wheels. Many of the components (such as the bells and balls that hang from the silver ankle-chains so beloved of Kutchi women) are now stamped by a mechanical press. There are also rolling mills, through which wire of a variety of gauges is put, although the gauge may be adjusted by pulling the wire through a draw-plate with a pair of pliers. The worker has to use his feet in order to do this, and will also need a colleague to assist him.

A street in a north-Indian jewelry bazaar.

Retail jewelers commission virtually all the work produced by the craftsmen, who divide the labour amongst themselves. Although the goods on show are from diverse sources – Australian gun-metal beads cut and faceted in Bombay, Surat, Ahmedabad or Rajkot, Rajkot cast and enamelled jewelry, enamelled boxes and *surahis* from Nathdwara – as much as 70 per cent is made in the vicinity for the local market. Anklets for the Muslim herders in the arid salt-flats of Banni Kutch and for the semi-nomadic Rabari shepherds are beaten out of low-grade silver bars, given a diamond-headed knob at each end, bent on a mandrel and then engraved with a floral and vegetal pattern. This is simple work, sold mainly for the value of the weight of metal.

In the manufacture of ankle-chains, first of all silver wire of the required gauge is wound into a spring-like coil, which is then cut along its length with a pair of shears, creating a large number of jump rings. These are then threaded onto an iron rod ready for use, and a simple link chain is made with the jump rings. (More complex chains can be created with different arrangements of S-shaped links and their variations on that form.) These chains, prefabricated findings, decorative bells, balls, or tiny heart-shaped pendants are laid out in the required order on an asbestos sheet and soldered with the aid of a blow-torch and a strand of silver solder wire. It is then pickled in a dilute solution of sulphuric acid and finally washed in a soapy dish. In Kutch, the finished silver is cleaned by dusting it in calcium powder.

Kutch is noted for its fine goldcraft, which includes some filigree work. Gold coins are reputedly used as base material to guarantee the quality of the metal, although in each jewelry-making centre there is always an assayer, with his assortment of little furnaces and crucibles on hand to analyze the relative purity of the metal. Some items are embellished using the ancient method of granulation. With this technique, tiny granules of gold or silver are prepared to the correct gauge and checked for size on another, fish-shaped gauge kept at close reach. The craftsman holds the granules in the palm of one hand which has been made slightly sticky with paraffin. Then, using tweezers, he carefully applies the granules in circular, triangular or diamond-shaped patterns onto the ornament. These granules and any cylindrical housings for the chips of semi-precious stones to be added later are all heated by a flame from a little oil lamp. He blows on the lamp using a short J-shaped blow-pipe known as a *bhagna*, which narrows as it descends from the mouth, giving a powerful and concentrated flame. The work is held on either a thin tin tray, a sheet of asbestos fibre, or the traditional low conductive plate of dried mud and cow-dung. The components of a fine and complex gold necklace are first laid out on a slightly sticky rubber pad in a traditional pattern or design taken from a Calcutta or Jaipur pattern book. Any piece of jewelry that is to be engraved or set with gems is always first placed firmly in a bed of lacquer.

Kutch is famous for the variety and intricacy of its jewelry, made to adorn with peacock-spendour not only the rich urban elite but also the many different tribes of semi-nomadic herders. Their conical or semi-spherical gold earrings are first punched out into a circular fretwork, then hammered into shape on a doming-block and set in the middle with a flake of red stone. At the back a cylindrical fastener is positioned centrally, into which is set a twist of wire or a screw fastening. The earrings pierce the middle cartilage of the ear, and are so heavy that they make it droop. Smaller versions of these are used as nose rings by women of the Kanbe farming caste and the Muslim herders of Banni Kutch, who also wear the *hansli* torque made of coiled spring-like wire.

Most of the richer, married women of western and southern India will wear the *mangal sutra* – a gold pendant hanging from a necklace of black gun-metal and gold beads – as a symbol of their marital status. With increasing prosperity, sophistication and urbanization, gold has become more popular.

As the wearing of jewelry by Indian women is both a social and religious requirement, jewelry-making is still prevalent throughout India, although now it is increasingly mechanized. As a craft industry, it is probably only second in importance to textile manufacture. Fewer items of fine jewelry are now being made in the little backstreet workshops of Indian towns, however, and a growing number of goods on display are the mass-produced, rather tawdry baubles that are made in such places as Rajkot. Yet quality is still being maintained at both ends of the social scale, for the richer Indians, although not adverse to innovation, demand finely crafted work for their money, while the poorer tribal and pastoral castes require the upkeep of traditional standards of workmanship by virtue of their intrinsic conservatism.

A paste, glass and base metal earring, from Hyderabad, Andhra Pradesh.

60 RIGHT *Beaded necklaces worn by the Naga tribespeople of north-east India.*

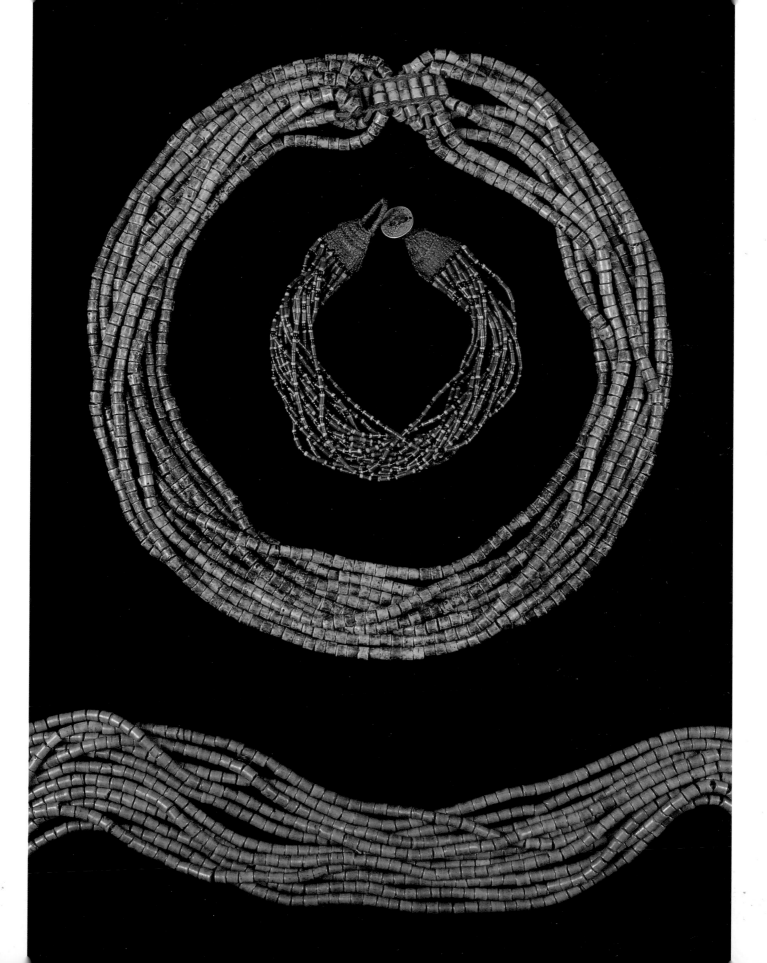

62 RIGHT *Thick ivory armlets are worn by men of many Naga tribes. They were originally made from the tusks of elephants killed locally, but by the 20th century, Angami Naga traders were buying African ivory in Varanasi and Calcutta. Highly desirable ornaments, they are indicative of high status – usually achieved through head-taking or feast-giving.*

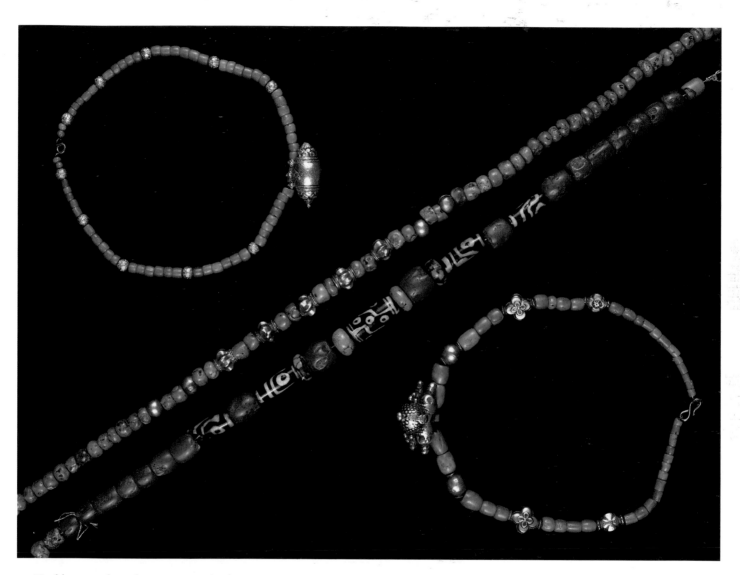

63 Necklaces such as these are worn in the Himalayas and Ladakh. From left to right: gold and coral beads; silver and coral beads; turquoise, coral and glass imitation dzi beads; and coral and silver beads.

64–6 LEFT *Silver 'tiger' anklets worn by the Bharward herder women of Saurashtra, Gujarat, either made locally or in Bombay (*TOP*); a woman's spiked silver bracelet, from Rajasthan (*CENTRE*); and armlets of silver and dyed cotton threads, known as* bajubandh, *which are worn by women of the Meena and Jat communities of Rajasthan (*BOTTOM*).*

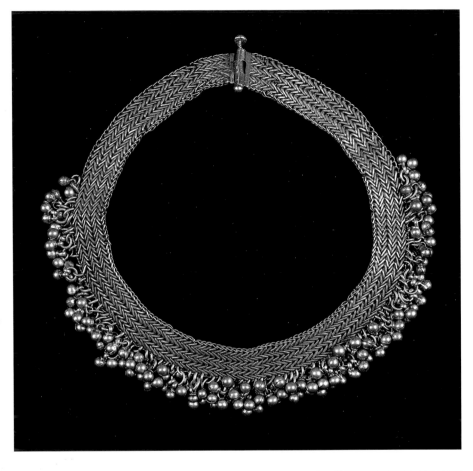

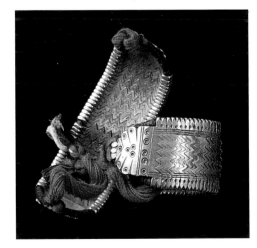

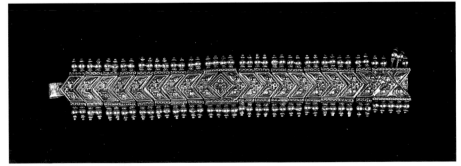

67 TOP *A necklace of linked silver chains and bells, from Maharashtra.*

68 ABOVE *A bracelet of linked silver repoussé elements, from southern India.*

69 Folk jewelry: a silver pendant of Balaji (Hanuman), worn by
many rural men in Rajasthan (top); a Banjara woman's coin and
base metal necklace (centre); and a necklace made up of men's
silver amulets, also from Rajasthan (bottom).

70 LEFT *A veiled Rajasthani Lohar woman adorned with bangles, necklaces, a nose-ring and* jhumka *earrings. Her neck, forearms and bosom are decorated with protective tattoos.*

71 RIGHT *Ox trappings of shells, seeds, glass beads and cotton tassels, hanging from a stall at a cattle fair in southern Maharashtra.*

72 FAR RIGHT *Silver anklets worn by a Rajasthani Lohar woman, who also bears traditional tattoos on her lower calves.*

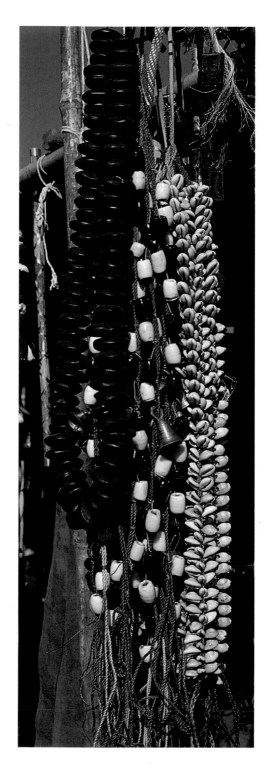

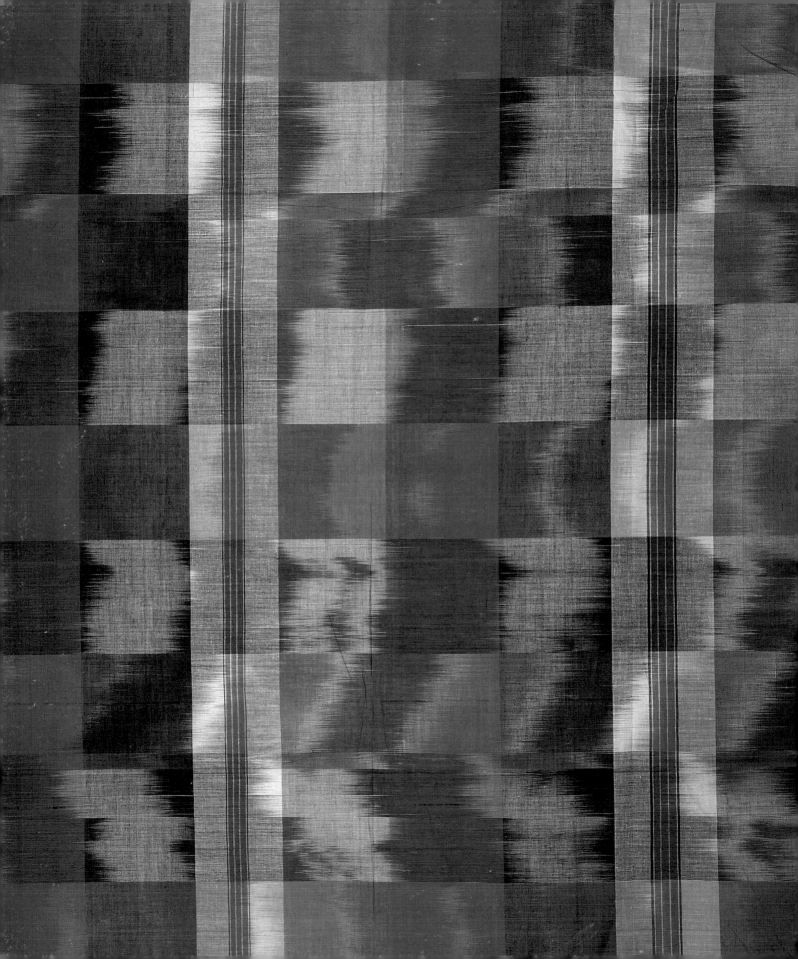

SILK, SATIN AND COTTON

Cotton and silk cloth, handwoven in all the different regions of this vast and varied land and often embellished with embroidery, metal threadwork, beads and even jewels, is fundamental to everyday life in India. It is through the cut, colour, texture and brilliance of their garments that Indians establish their exact position in a society so diverse and fragmented by religion, ethnicity, and the myriad divisions of caste that still so pervade an ostensibly secular land.

Having mastered the techniques of cotton processing in the days of the Indus Valley civilization, long before any other culture, India then assimilated the processes of silk manufacture, brought from China by way of Assam. Above all, however, the hallmark of Indian textile genius was its mastery of dyes and the use of mordants to make them fast and to form different colour combinations. This was to lead to the growth of an enormous textile industry with a vast geographical spread. From the coasts of Gujarat and Bengal, and from the Malabar and Coromandel littorals, ships sailed to Egypt, Arabia and China with cotton goods of such brilliance that all but the deepest Tyre-derived Roman purple and the finest Chinese silks were put to shame. Allied to this mastery of dyeing techniques was an astonishing range of textile skills and an enormous versatility of design. The resist techniques of block-printing, tie-dye and single- and double-ikat were practised often side-by-side with plain- and brocade-weaving to produce vividly patterned cloths of all kinds.

The flexibility with which Indian craftsmen were able to adapt their designs to suit any particular market, combined with their technical mastery, gave them the advantage they needed to make Indian textiles a vital component of both seaborne and overland Asian trading. The coming of the Europeans, following in the wake of Vasco da Gama, only intensified textile production and spread Indian cloth over a wider area, as by now it was not only vital to the spice trade but was also sold in West Africa, the Levant, the West Indies and the Americas. All this overseas trade had grown from firm foundations in its home land.

The courts of India – from the days of the Mauryas through to the splendours of the Mughal empire and beyond – were major patrons of the textile arts. The Mughals, indeed, set up special craft workshops (*kharkhanas*) whose sole criterion was excellence. This patronage was continued by the regional governors and the Rajput rulers, and also by the great temples and the rich merchants.

India's handloom industry, booming from European demand, exported vast amounts of muslins and chintzes in the 17th century, but was sorely injured by protectionist measures taken against it in the 18th, and in the next hundred years it was almost destroyed by its subjugation to the interests of the mechanized mills of

73 LEFT *A section of 'Madras check' loincloth patterned using the ikat technique and woven at Kanchipuram, Tamil Nadu.*

Lancashire and the colonial British. One of the side-effects of the American Civil War, however, was the establishment of vast commercial cotton plantations in India, which were intended to supply British mills deprived of American cotton. Subsequently textile mills were set up in Bombay and Ahmedabad. The handloom industry today is the child of past glories, a survivor of competition both from British and later from Indian mill-made cloth. After Independence, in the 1950s, old skills that had up until then been dying out were revived under the patronage of the government handicrafts boards.

Craft textile production serves both domestic and overseas markets, and although there is some overlap, the two are reasonably distinct. Of overwhelming importance for the home market is the sari. There is surely not a woman in India who does not have at least one handloomed sari, and more affluent women often have wardrobes full of them. The domestic demand supports a handloom industry in the states of Andhra Pradesh, Tamil Nadu and Karnataka; silk brocades are woven at Varanasi and Kanchipuram; *jamdani* weaves are produced in West Bengal; in central India Paithani and Maheshwari saris are famous for the subtlety of their brocades; Rajasthan is noted for the cotton saris woven at Kota; and in Tamil Nadu, at Kanchipuram and Tirukalukundrum village near Mamallapuram, the check cotton cloth lengths for use as mens' *lungis* and sarongs are produced.

Like the Coromandel coast (the home of chintz), the north-west of India is of special importance in the Indian textile world. It comprises the states of Gujarat, Rajasthan and parts of Madhya Pradesh, and has strong cultural links with the adjoining province of Sind, now in Pakistan. Much of this area was never directly ruled by the British, and consequently escaped the deleterious effects that the flood of imported mill-made cloth had on the rest of India; it also managed to retain its traditional social structure and maintain the many different craftsmen required to cater for its varied textile needs.

The former princely states of this region supported block-printers, tie-dyers and *patola* (double-ikat) as well as brocade weavers in its male-dominated, commercially orientated textile craft industry. The women of these areas, particularly those of the peasant and pastoralist castes of Kutch and the Saurashtran peninsula, are probably the world's foremost practitioners of folk embroidery. Each woman produces an intricately worked trousseau, often embellished with profuse mirror-work, for her marriage. With the help of her female relatives, she will make costumes for herself and for the bridegroom, as well as quilts, all manner of hangings for the home and even trappings for the domestic animals, using a variety of techniques including embroidery, appliqué, patchwork and beadwork. In a society made up of such complex caste divisions, the establishing of cultural identity is all-important, and it is seen as a mother's duty to pass down embroidery patterns and designs, customary stitches and colours, unchanged through the generations. Appliquéd wedding canopies, covers for piles of quilts and wall-hangings are made by women of the Rajput and Kathi ruling families and by some of the artisan castes. Visually stunning patchwork quilts and floor coverings are made in western Rajasthan and Sind by women of the Meghwal leather-working caste, while beadwork, bolster covers and wall decorations with the characteristic north-west Indian motifs of birds and flowers and religious icons are the domain of the landed Kathi families and the Mahajan merchant castes. The exquisite older examples use Venetian murano beads, the more recent work cruder Indian-made beads.

A doorway in Saurashtra is decorated with a beadwork toran *frieze and* chakla *squares. The girls are balancing pots topped with coconuts, each encased with beadwork, on their heads. These they will carry at their weddings.*

A *block-printed border design, from Kashmir.*

Akin to the folk embroidery of Gujarat and western Rajasthan is the *phulkari* work of Punjab. When a baby girl is born, her maternal grandmother will start to embroider her a wedding shawl. The shawl, known as a *phulkari*, is worked in floss silk from the back on red-brown handwoven cloth known as *khaddar*. The predominant colour is the gold of the ripening wheat harvest in Punjab's rich farmland, and the designs are usually geometric but can symbolize anything from suns and moons to playing cards. The woman will first prick up the outline of each section with a needle before it is worked in a direction that contrasts with the section adjacent to it, so that the juxtaposition of contrasting vertical and horizontal stitchery results in a splendid variety of textures, which is especially impressive when the light plays upon it.

Second in commercial importance to sari-weaving is the block-printing industry. With hand-carved blocks generally of *shisham* wood, articles of clothing and soft furnishings are created from hand- and mill-woven cloth, wherever there are skilled printers and water locally available for the repeated rinsings that are required. Patterns are floral and geometric rather than figurative, suggesting Muslim influence. Many of the designs, at least in north-west India, have Persian or Central-Asian origins.

The oldest block-printed Indian textiles to have survived, dating from the 14th century and earlier, were excavated in Fostat near Cairo. Their designs combine floral geometric patterning with a figurative element that is less common today. These textiles are most likely to have been Gujarati in origin; Gujarat, with its long coastline and many harbours, dominated the seaborne cotton trade, and is still today a major producer of block-print. Ahmedabad produces block-prints for the home and export market, particularly for East Africa, Ethiopia and the Yemen. Jetpur in Saurashtra is an important centre of commercial block-printing, while traditionally patterned cloth is printed at Deesa in northern Gujarat. *Ajrakh* cloth (Sindhi in origin) is printed at Barmer and at Dhamadka village in Kutch.

A *wood-block for printing fabric, being made in Pethapur, Gujarat.*

In Rajasthan, traditionally patterned cloth is block-printed in Barmer and Jaisalmer, and at Jodhpur and the nearby village of Salawas. Balotra is a major centre of commercial block-printing in Rajasthan, but the most important concentrations of the industry, both for export and for the home market, are at Bagru and Sanganer, near Jaipur. The latter two places traditionally specialized in fine floral Persian-derived prints, and the export market in yardage and finished goods has boomed in recent times, drawing many foreign buyers to Jaipur. Many screen-printers also live in both Bagru and Sanganer; screen-printing is an innovation that has made great inroads into the traditional block-printing market since 1970. Prints from Sanganer could traditionally be distinguished from those of Bagru as the Sanganer prints were worked on a white as opposed to a cream background. Udaipur and nearby Nathdwara are both block-printing centres, as are Jawad,

Tarapur, Mandasor and Bhairongarh just across the border in Madhya Pradesh. These places produce the floral repeat print that is so beloved of the Bhil and Banjara women.

One of the most striking yet economical ways for Indian women to dress is with tie-dye, known as *bandhani* in northern India (from which the English word 'bandanna' is derived). The most sophisticated *bandhani* is found in Kutch and in Jamnagar (Saurashtra). Kutch and Saurashtra still have a strong local market for *bandhani*, which keeps standards very high. The main concentrations of *bandhani*-work in Kutch are Bhuj, Anjar, Mandvi and Abrasa Taluka, the latter two producing the finest examples. Jamnagar, however, is the commercial centre for tie-dye in Gujarat. Much of the tying is done in Kutch and the dyeing, or sometimes only its final stages, in Jamnagar. The waters of its river are supposed to help produce a particularly brilliant shade of red.

The main colours used in the *bandhani* of this region are yellow, green, red and black – lighter colours are always dyed before the darker ones. The cloth may be the finest silk (the best *bandhani* is done on silk, for the weddings of the Khatri dyers' own daughters) or rough wool, but usually it is very permeable muslin which is folded in four before the tying process commences. This is supervised by the head of the family, but all the members, including the women and children, are involved. Those who actually tie the cloth grow a long nail on the little finger of the left-hand, or wear a ring with a little blunt spike on it, with which they push the layers of cloth upwards from underneath to form a tiny peak. Some details of colouring are spot-dyed: yellow dots are often daubed with blue to make green, for example. Dyers in Kutch and Saurashtra commonly work with three or four different dye baths, but in Rajasthan only one or possibly two are used; here, many of the additional colours are spot-dyed, which makes the process much easier. The main centres are Jaipur and Jodhpur, where much of the production is not only for the internal Indian market but also for export, so speed of production is of the essence. On the other hand, Barmer *bandhani* (usually a pattern of white or yellow dots on a deep madder-red background) and the brightly coloured *bandhani* of Sikar district in the Shekhawati region of Rajasthan are very popular locally. *Bandhani* is even made in the south, at Madurai in Tamil Nadu. The workers who are of Saurashtran origin generally produce patterns of fine spiralling dots in a single colour on a deep red ground.

Leheria is an interesting variant on the tie-dye theme that is practised in Jodhpur and Jaipur. Lengths of very permeable muslin are rolled from one corner to the opposite selvedge, bound tightly at intervals and then dyed in various dye baths. The ties are then undone and the process repeated by rolling the adjacent corner towards the other selvedge and repeating the tie-dye process. The end result is a very long and light turban cloth with a diagonally chequered pattern.

Ikat is the technique whereby the any number of warp or weft threads (sometimes both) are tied with dye-resistant materials to create a pattern before the weaving begins. There are three main centres of ikat production in India, Gujarat, Orissa and Andhra Pradesh. In Patan, Gujarat, two high-caste Jain families still weave the world-renowned silk *patola* double-ikat. This wonderfully fine and complex, brilliantly coloured fabric was once woven in many places in western India, and was India's leading textile export. Highly prized and much imitated, it was traded throughout South-East Asia. The tying and dyeing of the warps and

A kalamkari *representation of Arjuna, from Andhra Pradesh.*

wefts takes up to two months to complete, and then about a month to weave a 5-metre (6-yard) sari length on a simple, slightly angled loom. Throughout the weaving process, the weaver has to painstakingly adjust the weft threads with a metal pick to align them exactly with the warp threads. The patterning on a *patola* cloth is formed by this precise combination of differently dyed sections of warp and weft. Rajkot in Saurashtra produces single ikat, and compound ikat (which are sections of both warp and weft ikat, but they are not combined together). Some of the ikat-work in Rajkot imitates *patola*, and these imitations are far cheaper than the Patan originals, which have always been extremely expensive.

Orissa, cut off from outside influences for centuries by its thickly forested hills, produces the finest Indian ikat outside Patan, mainly at Nuapatna near Cuttack, and at Sambalpur and Barpali near the Madhya Pradesh border. The Meher weavers at Sambalpur and Barpali produce the finest work, often tying only three or four picks at a time; at present, they seem to be dominating Orissan production. Orissa exports to the rest of India, but benefits particularly from its strong local market. Most Orissan women wear local ikat saris, and the men may often be seen in an ikat *lungi* (sarong) or scarf.

A detail from a kalamkari *cloth made in Andhra Pradesh, depicting Rama.*

The most export-orientated ikat area in India is Pochampalli and its neighbouring villages, near to the city of Hyderabad in Andhra Pradesh. Its expert practitioners in the tying and weaving of ikat cloth originally came from Chirala in eastern Andhra Pradesh. It is here that the famous *telia rumals* are woven; these are alizarin-dyed double- and compound-ikat squares, which carry a characteristic smell of oil (used as a fixative*). Telia rumals* were once popular in those Muslim parts of India that became Pakistan in 1947, and also in the Middle East and Burma. Sadly, all these markets have long since vanished and the weavers have been reduced to abject penury. In Pochampalli, on the other hand, the ikat industry has gone from strength to strength. Originally confining themselves to the embellishment of simple sari borders and *lungis* with ikat decoration, the merchants and co-operatives have now developed a whole range of designs, drawing freely on *patola* and Orissan patterns, and producing yardage that is an excellent imitation of ikat from Japan, Guatemala or Bokhara. The product is well suited to the Western clothing and furnishing market, at which it is aimed. Both the private merchants and the co-operative managers are innovative and enterprising, maintaining a prosperous industry with relatively well-paid and contented workers.

The beautiful wax resist and painted chintzes of India's south-eastern Coromandel coast, with their eclectic designs of chinoiserie floral displays and even European motifs are sadly long gone. All that remains is the *kalamkari* ('penwork') of Masulipatnam and Kalahasti in Andhra Pradesh. The textiles at Masulipatnam are largely block-printed with some areas of the wax resist applied with a *kalam* (pen). Masulipatnam *kalamkari* was for a long time mainly exported to Iran, with which the ruling Shia princes of Golconda had strong links. In the 1920s Shah Reza Pahlavi prohibited this trade to protect Iran's indigenous industry, and production in Masulipatnam went into decline. It was revived in the 1950s by the efforts of the All-India Handicrafts Board and now has a healthy market producing furnishing cloth and bed-covers that sell throughout the subcontinent. Hand-painted *kalamkaris* have a long history of production at many places in the Tamil and Telegu areas of south-eastern India. These also experienced steep decline, and apart from one family at Sickiniakenpet (Tamil Nadu), the only remaining *kalamkari* centre is the temple town of Kalahasti in south-east Andhra Pradesh, near Madras. Here, the craftsmen only work part-time, drawing out vivid Hindu and sometimes Christian tableaux, and even company logos.

'*Mashru*', the name for mixed silk and cotton weaves, is derived from an Arabic word meaning 'permitted'. According to Islamic tradition, orthodox Muslim men were not allowed to wear silk next to the skin. *Mashru* fabric has silk (now often viscose) warps and cotton wefts, but as it is warp-faced, only the cotton wefts of the finished cloth would touch the skin. *Mashru* thus observed religious dictates while displaying a permissible amount of ostentation. It is decorated with warp stripes, and sometimes small areas of ikat. Before weaving any ikatted sections of warp threads can be manipulated to form arrow-head patterns. *Mashru* used to be woven in many places in India, especially at Hyderabad, Thanjavur, and Tiruchchirapalli in the south. Now it is woven between Bhuj and Mandvi (Kutch) and at Azamgarh (Uttar Pradesh). It is mainly used for decorative trimmings on garments and other textiles by Hindu farmers and pastoralists, and tribals.

The beautiful vale of Kashmir has always been famed for its craftsmanship. The weaving of tapestry shawls was first introduced into the valley from Turkestan by Zain Ul-Abdin, the ruler of Kashmir, in the 15th century. Production benefited from the patronage of the Mughal courts and local governors, and the shawls, with their combination of floral magnificence and restraint, attained a level of excellence that was never surpassed. The collapse of the Mughal empire left many weavers unemployed, but manufacture was saved by the enormous increase in demand from Europe, where the shawls had become fashionable in the latter part of the 18th century. At the beginning of the 19th century, foreign entrepreneurs started to commission shawls, particularly for the French market, adapting the designs to suit European taste. As the century progressed, these foreign adaptations became increasingly complex.

The European market was to collapse in 1870 owing to a combination of factors, including changing tastes and competition from European imitations such as Paisley shawls, but the prime cause was the economic prostration of France, catastrophically defeated by Prussia in the war of 1870. The Kashmiri weavers either left the valley for Punjab or tried to stave off penury and starvation by producing embroidery for the new tourist market aimed at British officers on furlough. Kashmir shawls are now embroidered by professional men, and there is a healthy Indian demand for *kurtas* (loose shirts) and table linen, as well as shawls.

The weaving of *jamawar* (tapestry) shawls has been restarted at Basohli in Himachal Pradesh, and the Kulu valley is an important centre for the weaving of woollen shawls with chequered tapestry-woven borders. Here, as in Kashmir, floral patterned woollen socks and jumpers are knitted.

India has a long and famous tradition of weaving magnificently decorated brocaded textiles. Every woman in India yearns for a Benares, Bangalore or Kanchipuram silk brocade sari for her wedding. Once they were woven at many places; in Gujarat, for instance, fine *kinkhab* silk and metal thread brocade was produced in Ahmedabad, Jamnagar and Surat until the Second World War. *Kinkhab* and fabrics akin to them were also woven at Hyderabad and Aurangabad (now the only place making the floating-weft fabric *himroo*). Tanda and Faizabad near Lucknow, and Murshidabad in Bengal, home of the famous Baluchar saris, were also once noted centres for brocade weaving.

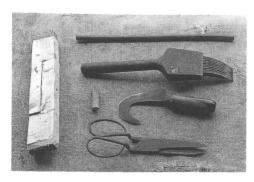

A selection of tools used for the hand-weaving of carpets.

Butta cones, used in Kashmiri embroidery patterns.

Varanasi (still often also known as Benares) has been India's primary brocade-weaving centre for many years. One of the oldest continuously inhabited cities in the world, it consists of a warren of streets leading to the temples and burning and bathing ghats down by the sacred Ganges. The weaving workshops are merely extensions – at any floor level – to the family home, where the weavers work at frame looms under an electric light. The complicated system of heddles is lifted either by a young assistant using the traditional *naksha bandha* (a complex arrangement of looped cords that are hanging above and attached to the heddles), or by the Jacquard method of punched cards. Designs vary over the years, as one fashion succeeds another, but there is a continuous demand for hunting scenes, flower and bird patterns, and dancing women.

Jamdani ('woven air') is the weaving tradition of Bengal. *Jamdani* textiles are discontinuous extra-weft fabrics of gauze-like muslin in which areas of detail are created by winding thread around the warps using small bobbins or pieces of card. The supplementary wefts are not taken all the way across the fabric, from one selvedge to the other, but restricted to each distinct section of patterning. *Jamdani* were traditionally woven at Dacca and Murshidabad, but since Partition in 1947 those produced in West Bengal, where they are known by the trade name of 'Tangail' (a village outside Dacca) are made by weavers who originally came from Bangladesh.

Bengal has a delightful tradition of embroidery and quilting known as *kantha* or *nakshi kantha*. In the frugal manner of most rural peoples, village women would quilt together layers of old saris or *dhotis*, which in Bengal had a plain white ground, using red, green or black threads with which the sari borders were decorated. The quilting stitches outlined the patterns to be filled in with embroidery stitches or often formed the very patterns themselves. Quilts, wedding mats, eating cloths, bags and wraps for mirrors and jewelry were all quilted and embroidered, often by the poorer villagers for the family of the local *zamindar* (landlord). Motifs were drawn from the rural landscape, boats and marine life, and sometimes represented temple festival carts, circus entertainers and even historical figures such as Queen Victoria and Lenin. *Kanthas* were embroidered all over Bengal west of the river Meghna, and crude but rather dramatic ones were made in Bihar, although the main centres were in what is now Bangladesh. *Kantha*-making died out in the 1920s, but was revived in both Bangladesh and West Bengal in the 1970s. Even though the old designs were used, they somehow lacked the spontaneity of the older pieces. *Kanthas* are now embroidered near Calcutta and Shantiniketan, with figurative, commonly Hindu religious and folk motifs, often using silk threads.

Chikan-work is a kind of white-work wherein predominantly floral designs are worked using untwisted cotton, silk or viscose on the surface of the fabric. The *chikan*-work embroidery of Lucknow is supposed to have originated as an imitation of a certain type of *jamdani* weaving. Most Lucknow *chikan*-work is now found on the necklines and cuffs of cheap thin muslin *kurtas* and chemises destined for the home and export market.

Indian floor coverings are mostly flat-woven, and usually made of cotton rather than pile-woven wool. Cotton flat-weaves are known as dhurries, and are woven not only for floors but also for spreading over the string mesh of the *charpoy* (bed) used in rural India, upon which the bedding is laid. The finest dhurries

A 17th-century Mughal carpet, woven in Agra.

were woven in Indian prisons between 1880 and 1920. Their splendour is now a thing of the past, although the Jats of Haryana produce striking geometric dhurries of white lozenges and triangles, often set on a blue ground, and at Nikodar near Jullundur, in Punjab, weavers specialize in figurative designs. Commercial dhurrie-making is found all over India, but at Panipat near Delhi, Jodhpur, and at Bhavani near Salem (Tamil Nadu) in particular. Wonderfully vibrant dhurries known as *jamkhana* are made by Muslim weavers at Navalgund in Karnataka. Their most famous design is the *paggadi*, featuring peacocks surrounding a cross-shaped *parcheesi* game board, supposedly derived from the Adil Shahi court at nearby Bijapur.

Knotted-pile carpets were introduced into India by the Mughals, who had enormous carpets of fine quality woven in workshops at Agra and Lahore. British carpet companies, starting with Ziegler in Kashmir in the 19th century, began making hand-knotted carpets in Kashmir, Agra and Lahore. Now production is concentrated in Mirzapur and Bhadohi, in Uttar Pradesh, which together account for over 80 per cent of the output, and in Jaipur in Rajasthan; the carpet industry, however, has a tendency to move anywhere where labour is cheap, especially into tribal areas. Carpets woven in Uttar Pradesh are rather coarse, but Agra and particularly Jaipur specialize in finer carpets (144 knots per square inch is the normal grade). Designs are taken from classical Persian carpets. The 'map-reader' sings out the design and colours to be used from a cartoon (there are several boys doing this for different looms within one factory) and the weaver follows his instructions. Production is overwhelmingly export-orientated, aimed mainly at Germany and the United States.

The hand-production of textiles is India's foremost craft industry, employing many thousands of men and women all over the country. Export demand may fluctuate with the fashion for the 'ethnic' look in Western countries. The home market, however, is strong and constant – hand-weavers, block-printers, dyers and embroiderers are kept ever busy, providing textiles for the urban masses as well as for the specific requirements of traditional local communities.

74 RIGHT *Detail of a* rumal (cover) *from Kashmir. It is embroidered in chain-stitch with Persian-inspired human and celestial figures, birds and* butta *cones.*

75 *A temple hanging from Kumbhakonam district, Tamil Nadu. The motifs worked in appliquéd felted wool depict Ganesh mounted on his rat, and Subrahmanya with his consorts astride his peacock. At festival times, silver images of these deities are paraded around the temple 'tank' at Kumbhakonam and then ritually immersed in the water.*

76 *A brightly patterned* jamkhana dhurrie *woven at Nawalgund, Karnataka, to a traditional pattern which, according to local weavers, dates back to the days of the Adil-Shahi kings of Bijapur (1490–1686). The central cross-shaped motif represents* a parcheesi *or* chaupad *gameboard, from which the English game of ludo originates.*

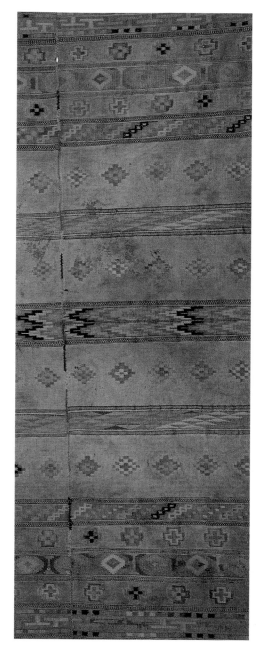

77 BELOW *Detail of a shawl from Kulu or Kinnaur valley. The skills used to weave such shawls, traditionally of pashmina wool, were brought to Kulu from Kinnaur over a century ago, and an important industry has developed, now using many kinds of wool.*

78 *An embroidered* choli *(backless bodice) from Chamba, Himachal Pradesh.*

79 *Detail of a block-printed cotton* jajam *(floor-spread) from Ahmedabad, Gujarat.*

80 *The corner of a fringed patchwork* rumal *(cover) from Gujarat. The* kinkhab *brocade fabric was woven in Ahmedabad before Independence in 1947.*

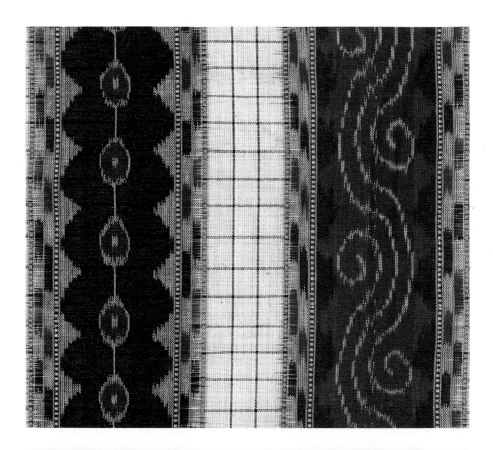

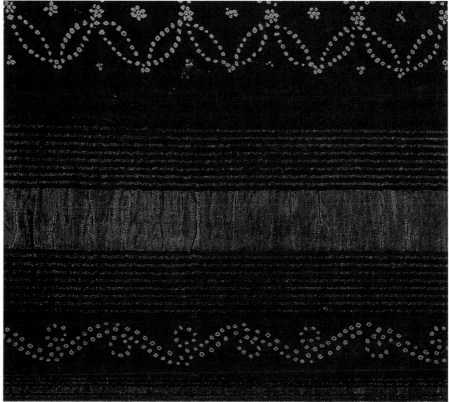

81 *Warp-ikat yardage from Barpalli, Orissa.*

82 *The tie-dyed and brocaded border of a wedding sari from Jamnagar, Gujarat.*

83 *Ox and buffalo-hide sandals known as* chappals, *made near Kolhapur, Maharashtra. They are dyed black with diesel oil.*

84 *Men's leather slippers decorated with metal-thread embroidery, made in Jodhpur, Rajasthan.*

85 OPPOSITE *Shoes of plaited jute and crocheted wool, from Himachal Pradesh.*

CHAPTER VI

MINIATURES
TO PAPIER-MÂCHÉ

Indian drawings and paintings survive from prehistoric times but they are difficult to place in any firm sequence; it is difficult, too, to understand the impulses at work. How much was it magic, how much mimicry that inspired those early drawings? One thing is clear: they were the ancestors of much present-day folk art which, generally with religious overtones, still flourishes in rural India, and even intrudes into the urban tower block! But India is better known for its sophisticated paintings illustrating palm-leaf manuscripts or, later, the Mughal, Rajput and Pahari miniatures inspired by Persian art. There was also another, more powerful Islamic influence which shunned the figurative but brilliantly exploited geometric and plant forms. That the European Renaissance left its mark is hardly remarkable, for the Portuguese were in India before the Mughals. The most vigorous progeny of the Mughal and Western synthesis is the kitsch style so common in poster art.

The earliest traces of Indian painting are preserved in caves and rock shelters occupied in prehistoric times. Sophisticated art, too, survives in caves, in the Buddhist rock-carved monasteries of the middle of the first millennium AD, such as Ajanta (Maharashtra) and Bagh (Madhya Pradesh). A true sequence of paintings begins with 11th-century Jain (Gujarat) and Buddhist (Bihar, Bengal) manuscripts. Jain figures, slender-waisted and in sharp-featured profile (although both eyes are shown) are drawn on a ground of solid colour.

Islam brought new ideas. Although mostly Sunnis, to whom figurative art had become taboo, the invaders fell in the Persian cultural orbit. The Persians, Shias, were enthusiastic patrons of figurative miniatures and inspired the court art of Malwa (north Madhya Pradesh) and the Deccan states (Maharashtra/Karnataka). Then came the Mughals. In 1555 Humayan, returning from exile in Persia, brought painters. His son, Akbar, made them the nucleus of a workshop which, encouraged by his interest and that of Jahangir after him, flourished. Hindus joined the atelier, bringing their own idioms, and European art, introduced by the Jesuits, was much admired and copied. It inspired the Rajput schools which grew up in the Rajasthani courts. Their rulers intermarried with princes of the Punjab Hills (Himachal Pradesh) and a further school, Pahari ('of the hills'), was born. This included the Kangra atelier, prominent in the late 18th and early 19th centuries. The 19th century brought universal decay. European realism flooded the country, often in the form of cheap prints. Patronage now came not only from rulers and merchants but also from the wealthy British.

From the 1850s, attempts were made to stem the decline in indigenous art and craft. Colleges teaching craft skills were founded by private individuals, British or

86 LEFT *Sea shells used to contain ground mineral pigment for miniature painting, from Kishangarh, Rajasthan.*

Indian, some by enlightened princes and others by public subscription. Today, the craft element in these colleges has been eclipsed by that of design and fine art. Self-conscious efforts to relate these to their Indian roots tend to be withered by the all-pervasive rays of the Western cultural sun.

Far removed from the courts and cities, in degree if not distance, folk painting thrived. It passed through the colonial experience little scathed, still retaining its associations with marriage and religious rituals. The artists were often women, their canvas the mud-and-dung finish of walls and floors, their paint ochres, lime, rice paste and, increasingly, bright poster colours.

Many Brahmin and Kayasth women of Madhubani district (Bihar) are particularly accomplished, decorating houses for marriages and feasts with bright, lively deities, most popularly Krishna and his beloved Radha. The form of each figure is a highly stylized profile of the face and feet whilst the body often faces the viewer. Characteristically, the outlines are drawn as a double line with diagonal hatching between them. During the Bihar famine of 1964–5 some of these women began to reproduce their pictures on paper. At home the painters use the frayed end of a piece of bamboo twig or rag on a stick as a brush. For one form of decoration, *aripana* (the drawing of circular mandalas common throughout India for domestic ceremonies), the woman uses her finger to 'write', as she herself describes it, the powerful Tantric symbols she requires.

A Rajawar painted mud doorway, Madhya Pradesh.

The murals of the Warli tribals of the coastal region of southern Gujarat and northern Maharashtra are also now commercially painted, often executed on specially prepared softboard. Typically, these pictures show multitudes of tiny human forms hunting, dancing or cultivating the land. They rely more on line than colour, usually being drawn in white rice paste to prepare for specific festivals or family events. Further north, in northern and eastern Gujarat, *pithora* pictures dominated by long-necked horses still decorate some step-wells and houses of the Bhil tribal folk.

The custom of painting on mud walls is widespread, but it is usually confined to certain castes. The Sawai Madhopur and Bharatpur districts of Rajasthan are rich in white figurative painting as well as textural patterns worked into the wet mud. To the west, beyond Jaisalmer and in the Banni area of Kutch (Gujarat) desert cottages often boast abstract or figurative painting, sometimes coloured in pastel ochres. Patterns of hand-prints intended to stem the advance of the evil eye are common in rural areas. Wealthy rural communities are also involved in this folk tradition. At Diwali, the Festival of Light, the most skilled women in many north-Indian households will be expected to paint a geometric representation of Lakshmi, goddess of fortune, low on the wall of a room, to be the focus of family worship on the day.

A detail of a Warli mural of a palace depicting the legend of the princess and the crane.

British domination had a major impact on Hindu religious art. Cheap prints and colourful picture labels aimed at the Indian market inspired mimicry. They gave rise to prints of gods depicted as those same youthful androgynous folk beloved of Western Christianity, and now popular throughout India.

In Thanjavur (Tamil Nadu) a single family preserves an individual school of painting which, whilst integrating foreign elements, continues an old tradition expressed in an original technique. Thin cardboard is glued onto a board of *pilla* wood, and over this a sheet of calico. On this surface a paste of gum made from ground tamarind seeds and powdered stone is spread. When this is dry the outline of a picture is sketched in crayon. It is a characteristic of these paintings that decorative materials are used to embellish them – in the very best work gold leaf and semi-precious stones may be used but, more commonly, these are replaced by foil and coloured glass. The gold leaf or foil is glued over selected parts of the sketch, followed by the real or imitation gems. It is only at this stage that painting begins, using strong primary colours and starting with the background. Finally, the main figures are added and the details completed. Today the hand-ground natural colours have been replaced by factory-produced pigments.

At other major religious centres, painters still compete with the sellers of popular prints, turning out pictures of the local deity for sale to pilgrims. Nathdwara (Rajasthan) is famous for its *pichhwai*, which are large paintings on cloth portraying Sri Nathji, a powerful icon of Krishna clad in his various costumes, as well as miniatures on paper or card. Most are, as they always were, low-quality, cheap souvenirs. The style probably developed soon after the idol, fleeing iconoclasts, reached its present home.

Orissa, isolated from Muslim invasion and distant from imperial courts, has retained a pre-Islamic style of religious art that has altered little over the years. In Puri and its surroundings *patachitra* are still turned out for the millions of pilgrims who flock to the great Jagannath Temple. These are cloth paintings executed on a leather-like surface comprising layers of old cotton cloth glued together with a gum made of ground tamarind seed. Apart from the three idols of the temple – Jagannath, lord of the universe, Subhadra, his sister, and Balbhadra, his brother – the painters depict various religious subjects in a sharp-featured ritualized form. The painters are called *chitrakar* and belong to a skilled Sudra community who sculpt, carve wood, stone and ivory and cast metal as well as paint. Certain individuals will specialize in one particular field and in Puri, Raghurajpur and Danda Sahi some of these devote themselves to *patachitra* work. The stiff surface is primed with white chalk mixed with tamarind glue, and then burnished using a round stone. On this, the artist sketches his drawing with a fine brush, in red ochre or turmeric. A skilled *chitrakar* works without reference to any sketches, reproducing the familiar compositions and figures that comprise popular Hindu religious art. When the layout is complete he fills in the red background colour before embarking on the bodies and clothes of the figures, each colour being added in turn. The final stage involves outlining faces and jewelry in close detail and accentuating sections of the picture with black lines. The finished article is varnished to protect it from dirt and damp.

The larger *patachitras* today most commonly portray Vaishnavite themes, often the ten *avatars* of Vishnu. One type of screen, the *ansarapati*, is produced for the procession of Jagannath through Puri. Hindu months are lunar, divided into a 'bright' (waxing) half and 'dark' (waning) half, and preparation for this painting begins on the third lunar day of the 'bright fortnight' in Vaisakha month (April to May). During his work the *chitrakar* can only eat once a day (in the afternoon), must avoid meat and intoxicants, and has to abstain from sexual intercourse. This regime must be followed until he completes the painting – the eyeballs are the last part to be finished.

The *chitrakar* uses a similar technique to decorate wooden articles such as the *jantaka pedi*, a dowry box. The woodwork is covered with cloth steeped in tamarind gum and, when dry, primed with chalk and more gum; on this surface,

A pata *painting of Durga, from Uttar Pradesh.*

pictures from the myths of Krishna and Rama are painted. They once also illustrated palm-leaf manuscripts with fine line drawings etched with a steel stylus. The leaf comes from a type of palmyra palm known as *khar-tad*. Elsewhere, the tradition of religious writings on palm leaf faded away during the 18th century. In Orissa it continues, albeit in a degenerate form. The style of the figures, shown in profile, pointed-nosed, long-eyed, with rounded bodies but sharp, angular limbs, is similar to that of medieval Gujarati and Rajasthani work.

Another form of religious painting was executed purely to illustrate a narrative story for recital. The Pabuji *pad*, on a cloth screen some 5 metres (over 16 feet) long by 1.3 metres (over 4 feet) high, depicts the miraculous life of the god-hero Pabuji Rathor, in little-altered, mid-18th-century style. Painted by hereditary craftsmen in and around Shahpura (Rajasthan), it is carried by itinerant bards. The narrator sings the story in front of the screen whilst his wife points to each episode as he describes it. When worn out, the *pad* was ritually destroyed, and consequently its early evolution is obscure. Now it is painted almost entirely as a curio, as few men still perform. Other such Rajasthani screens tell of similar figures such as Ramdevji, and Dev Narayan, whose story has been copied onto the walls of shrines dedicated to him in Shahpura.

A ganjifa *playing card, made in Puri, Orissa.*

These screens – the props of story-tellers – were widespread before film, and television reduced them to collectors' pieces. In West Bengal and neighbouring Bihar there are still a few itinerants, such as the *jadu pata* and *patidar*, who illustrate stories with hand-painted pictures. Some had their pictures painted on wood. The *kavadh*, a combination of a cupboard and a screen which unfolds to reveal Vishnu and his incarnations, is still made near Chittor in Rajasthan. Those made for story-tellers were some 80 centimetres (about 30 inches) high, but today small copies are made for tourists.

Cloth paintings were produced for religious rituals, to be displayed at certain festivals. At the northern tip of the country, in Ladakh, where Tibetan Buddhism flourishes, and in parts of Himachal Pradesh, where Tibetan refugees have settled, *thankas* are painted on cloth, often showing the Buddha and the Wheel of Life.

Miniature painting as a living art faded with the 19th century. Now Delhi, Varanasi, Udaipur and Jaipur have become centres for latter-day miniaturists working on paper, cloth and ivory, although this is now difficult to acquire thanks to animal protection legislation, and artists rely either on recycling old ivory or on a busy black market. They generally use thin sheet, often made up of several carefully joined pieces, and smooth the surface with cuttlebone, a very soft natural abrasive, before drawing a pencil sketch. When the outline is satisfactory it is inked in with a fine brush then, after drying, washed over to soften the lines. The ground colour is filled in first, starting at the top, and the buildings, plants and animals added. Human figures follow; the faces, so easily damaged by the touch of a sweaty hand, are left till last. Acrylic paints are generally used, but the best work calls for natural pigments. The technique of painting on paper is very similar but here the outline is softened by covering the surface with chalk.

South Asian and European playing cards probably spring from a common origin. Indian cards – *ganjifa* – are circular and come in sets of 96, 120 or 144 to accommodate 8, 10 or 12 different suits, as opposed to the four of the now-ubiquitous French pack. Each suit has two court cards: in the Mughal pack the raja and *diwan* (minister), and in the Hindu pack Rama, Krishna or another of the ten *avatars* (depending on the type of pack), and a *mantri* (minister). The remaining cards are numbered from one to ten. They are made along the lines of the Orissan *patachitra*, with several layers of glued cloth which is primed and then painted. Some craftsmen use a pounce, especially to reproduce the court cards, but the more skilled amongst them work freehand. The outlines are then filled in with colours mixed with gum. Traditional cards were still widely made in the 19th century, but the mass-produced French pack has now superseded them. Today, not many people outside Orissa use the old pack, although the cards are still made in Raghurajpur, Chitikigada and Parlakhemundi (Orissa), Sawantwadi (Maharashtra), Nirmal (Andhra Pradesh) and Bishnupur (Bengal). They are sold in brightly painted wooden boxes, as curios.

The technique of glass painting was imported from Europe. Widespread in the 19th century, the craft is now confined to a few practitioners in Kutch (Gujarat), Jaipur and Nathdwara (Rajasthan) and Thanjavur (Tamil Nadu), where the paintings were particularly intricate, and included bright foil with the background. The artist paints on the back of the glass, reversing the usual sequence – jewelry and facial features are applied first, then clothing, flesh and finally background. Buildings and furniture display British influence. Many of these pictures were religious, and they still feature in the *puja* room of traditional middle-class Tamil homes.

Building materials used in ancient Indian architecture were inimical either to the execution or the survival of wall-paintings. Temples came to be built of stone and, until the 16th century, Hindu domestic buildings were of wood or brick. There are a few remnants of murals in the north attributed to late Gupta times, such as the 5th-century paintings of Ajanta and Bagh, whilst in the south there are temple paintings dating back to the 13th century. The Mughal rulers expected their artists to work on plaster as well as cloth and paper. During the construction of Fatehpur Sikri in the 1570s, some buildings were covered with fine murals.

Akbar's great Hindu general, Man Singh, was Raja of Amber, his capital only 200 kilometres (124 miles) from Fatehpur Sikri. Soon murals in his country reflected the imperial style, these surviving in his memorial *chhatri* (domed cenotaph) of 1620, the Mughal capital at Bairat (1622), and Makhdoom Shah's tomb, Amber (*c.* 1625). Too little survives from earlier times for us to know whether the Mughals triggered a wave of wall painting or, as seems more likely, merely transformed a vigorous art.

Two techniques are widely used in wall-painting: 'Jaipur fresco' and tempera on dry plaster. With Jaipur fresco, the colours (usually ochres) are worked onto the damp surface, resulting in a highly polished surface remarkable for its tenaciousness. The tempera method was generally used inside buildings. The drawings were made on dry plaster, occasionally aided by pounce stencils for repetitive figures. The pigment was mixed with gum made from bones or plants as a binding medium. In Rajasthan the artists were generally masons or carpenters.

The demand for murals soared during the 19th century – the era of mercantile prosperity – and was concentrated particularly in Rajasthan, Punjab and Gujarat, the greatest display being in the Shekhawati region of Rajasthan. The popularity of painted walls continued well into the 20th century, although quality declined after the 1850s. Today figurative murals are generally confined to temples, painted in bright acrylic following the poster-art style. The sign-painter still produces huge

A detail from an 18th-century painted box depicting Vishnu riding an elephant, from southern India.

film hoardings on walls, cloth banners or metal sheets. In some states, particularly Punjab, Haryana and Kerala, there is a major demand for pictures on the chassis of trucks, buses and rickshaws. In Kerala the religious persuasion of the truck-owner is evident to all, for the back of his cab will be painted with a figure of Lakshmi, goddess of wealth, if he is a Hindu, or a chubby infant reading the Koran, palms heavenwards, if he is a Muslim. Christians prefer St George slaying the dragon.

An unusual domestic craft amongst womenfolk is the decoration of hands and feet with henna designs. A pulp of henna leaves is put into a cloth 'syringe' and a skilled woman will apply the pulp in a fine lacework designs from memory. The painted individual has to avoid using her hands for a couple of hours – a wonderful way to keep little girls out of mischief. When the henna is washed off the design remains imprinted on the skin and persists for several days. Tattooing is also quite widespread amongst the tribal communities. Bhil men, for example, often have blue designs at the corner of each eye whilst women may have blue-dotted arms. Far more ambitious tattoos are etched on the faces of tribesmen in Kerala and nomadic groups in Karnataka.

It is folk art that remains the most dynamic in modern India. There is the confidence of well-tried tradition, a confidence that also inspires the bright decorative work on vehicles and in temples. Sophisticated painting has yet to recover from the 19th-century collision with the West. Miniature painters have become copyists, harking back to a classic era; the art schools produce artists in the Western mould, individualists rather than craftsmen tied to patronage.

A Bhil youth adorned with light pigment to represent a leopard for a Holi festival procession in eastern Gujarat.

PAPER, PAPIER-MÂCHÉ, MASKS AND KITES

For many centuries, Indian writing and painting flourished using the dried leaves of the palmyra palm in place of paper. Their elongated shape dictated the form of the pre-Mughal native book, with the script and illustrations oriented parallel to the long axis of the page. Paper appeared as a luxury item manufactured for the writings and paintings of the wealthy before it finally replaced leaves. Only as it became more commonplace was enough waste generated for subsidiary crafts; of these, papier-mâché and kite-making became the most widespread.

The emperor Babur is said to have introduced paper-making into India, and during the 1520s he encouraged the establishment of an industry near Alwar (Rajasthan). Later, Kashmir became famous for the quality of its paper, particularly sought after by miniaturists. In 1728 the dynamic Maharaja Jai Singh II, founder of Jaipur city, attracted paper-makers to the business he set up in nearby Sanganer.

The paper is made from cotton waste and off-cuts reduced to pulp, which is transferred into large rectangular tanks. Two workers submerge a rectangular tray of fine mesh into the surface water and empty a mugful of pulp from the bottom of the tank into the water above the tray, which they agitate as it settles. The tray is lifted out and a piece of muslin is stretched over the sheet of pulp. It is then inverted and the muslin, with the sheet of pulp now on top of it, is added to a pile which is pressed, driving out most of the water. These sheets are peeled off the muslin and hung out to dry.

Much of the paper is decorative. Often the pulp is dyed, and a marbled effect can be achieved by mixing oil colour with turpentine and flicking it on the water's

A Bhil tattoo depicting a peacock.

surface so that it is caught on the pulp sheet as it is lifted out. Another trick is to introduce flower petals and grass into the pulp so that they feature in the finished sheet. There are also variants in the material used for the pulp. A fine paper can be made from silk off-cuts with lime added to the water to whiten it. Previously jute was an important raw material for the paper on which miniatures were painted, and there is still a small demand for this amongst painters.

Handmade paper is produced in Ahmedabad (Gujarat), Khuldabad, Jeandal, Jumnar and Pune (Maharashtra), Kalpi (Uttar Pradesh) and at the Aurobindo Ashram (Pondicherry) but the Sanganer units are probably the best known. When paper is used for craftwork it is machine-made from such materials as wood pulp and cloth waste. Papier-mâché is a flourishing craft, especially in the Kashmir valley where it developed in Mughal times as a side product of the paper industry there. The manufacture of the Kashmir valley has traditionally been controlled by Shia Muslims. In Indian papier-mâché, the paper is not usually pulped, merely soaked then pasted, layer on layer, over a mould. When the object is completed, a thin layer of chalk mixed with glue is traditionally applied to the surface, and burnished with a piece of agate, although nowadays this is often substituted by a commercial emulsion. The ground is painted with a mixture of pulverized tinfoil and glue, or even gold for the very best items, but for the highly commercial batch production, which has been the norm since at least the early 1970s, a background colour is painted on, which is usually black. Then the large floral outlines are applied and the colours and details are built up, stage by stage. Six to twelve colours are used. The final painting uses fine squiggly lines to fill in the blank spaces – sometimes a single animal hair is used as a brush. Last of all, the surface is varnished with two good coats of commercial lacquer.

There are a number of labour-saving techniques used in the production of cheaper items – sometimes, for example, pulped paper is placed between the layers to increase bulk. But increasingly, in Kashmir, paper is being replaced by cardboard. A great variety of objects are made, including trinket boxes, bowls, lamps and candle stands, trays and cases for pens. The real attraction of Kashmiri work is its fine painted decoration – an intricate *zamin* (ground) of little flowers set in vegetation against which are painted birds, mammals and huntsmen.

With Kashmir at its heart, the craft is very widespread throughout the country. It is used particularly in the making of masks, usually for religious rituals or performances. Often these are amateur products, put together for some annual festival to replace damaged stock. In parts of the south, particularly around Thanjavur, masks and even large figures are fashioned from papier-mâché; more famously, the Kathakali dancers of Kerala wear partial or complete masks, as well as headdresses, all made from papier-mâché.

In West Bengal both performers and professionals are involved in mask manufacture, principally for the 'Chho' performances (folk dance-dramas often illustrating episodes from the epics and common also to Bihar and Orissa). Here wooden masks are worn as well as papier-mâché ones, made by village carpenters and painted by a separate caste for tribal communities in the state. The Santhal tribes, for example, generally buy masks, whilst the Rakha and Lepcha communities normally make their own. Only in Purulia district is a variant of papier-mâché, with the addition of clay and old cloth, preferred. In the neighbouring state of Orissa, papier-mâché masks are produced in Puri and at Raghurajpur and

A peacock dance performed by a Kathakali dancer from Kerala. The costume is made of cloth and papier-mâché.

Jeypore, along with toys. Others made of *simuli* wood are made in Karagadia, Chikitigada, Belaguntha and Dharakote. These are coated with gummed cloth ready for painting. Large processional masks are fashioned from bamboo, the facial forms being moulded from a mixture of tamarind glue and either sawdust or rice husks.

The most widespread paper-craft product must be the kite. Kite-flying is not merely a child's pastime; it is also a competitive adult sport. Through much of north and central India demand reaches its peak for the festivals of Makar Sankranti (14 January), and in Punjab for Basant (11 February). Both these are traditional kite-flying days, taking an annual toll of people who fall from high vantage points, especially flat roofs, and motorcyclists who run into the taut strings. The aftermath is a vision of trees full of strange, bright blooms which are entrapped kites.

The basic Indian kite is a supported square of paper with either a *puchari* (a tail streamer) or a *chapat* (a squat triangular tail) attached to one corner, so that it has a diagonal axis. The paper used is varied, sometimes bearing portraits of popular film stars. Foil, cellophane and polythene are often used and recently bright paper rejected from factory packing or advertising. Because of the seasonal demand, the small permanent community of kite-makers is swelled by men from quite different vocations.

The frame is made up of pieces of split bamboo. Using a brown paper *farna* (template), the kite-maker cuts the paper, sometimes several layers at a time. He glues a splint and places it across a diagonal of the square. This is the *dadha*. Over and across it he bends, bow-like, another splint – the *käman* (bow) – which he glues to the two other corners. The hems of the paper are folded to reinforce the edges. The ends of the two splints are fixed more firmly in place by squares of glued paper, usually of a contrasting colour. This completes the kite. It only remains for the tail-streamer or a stubby little *chapat*, reinforced by a splint at each side, to be attached to the underside. Much of the kite-flying is combative, the aim being to sever as many kite strings as possible, sending the colourful kites drifting away over roof and street pursued by gangs of eager boys. The string is therefore important, especially at the festival season, and during the first fortnight of January men can be seen walking along beside great lengths of thread stretched between posts, to which they apply a mixture of gum, colour and powdered glass. The powdered glass turns the thread into a cutting edge.

Paper is used for many forms of decoration, especially at religious shrines and at marriages. The groom often arrives at the bride's house wearing a garland of banknotes. These, in mint condition, are painstakingly worked into rosettes and whorls, the denomination of the note indicating the affluence of the family.

Although the manufacture of handmade paper is a relatively small, threatened industry, reliant on an affluent middle-class and Western demand, factory production is vast and ever-growing, depleting the softwood forests. With paper waste and cardboard cheap and readily available, the papier-mâché industry, particularly in Kashmir, is only limited by demand. Apart from the masks, papier-mâché items are largely aimed at the tourist and overseas markets. Not so the kites, which are generally too fragile to travel far. Kite-flying remains a popular occupation for children and there is no sign of the annual kite festivals declining; this craft at least still appears to be thriving.

87 RIGHT *A wooden panel from Nirmal, Andhra Pradesh, painted in traditional Mughal-inspired patterns.*

88 LEFT *A cloth painting of the deity Jagannath, from Raghurajpur, Orissa. At the top and bottom of the central image are scenes from Krishna's life, including Krishna sucking the poisonous nipples of the demoness Putana.*

89 *A painting of Kamadhenu, half cow, half woman, goddess of boons and mother of all cattle. The image is painted on cloth pasted to wood and then coated with a mixture of gum and chalk; the jewelry and trappings are raised in low-relief using a special plaster and then coated in gold leaf. Thanjavur, Tamil Nadu.*

90 *Sri Nathji, the local idol of Krishna, painted on card. Such pictures are made as souvenirs for the many pilgrims who visit the important temple at Nathdwara, Udaipur district, Rajasthan. The idol was brought from Govardhan in the late 17th century to escape Mughal iconoclasts.*

91, 92 *Paintings on cloth of the Rajasthani folk deity Pabuji.* LEFT *Pabuji rides his black mare, Kesar Kalami, into battle against his enemy, the villain Jindrav Khinchi.* BELOW *Pabuji receives an offering from a village girl.*

93 RIGHT *A folk rendering of the elephant-headed god Ganesh, from Madhubani district, north Bihar. Such works were once exclusively wall decorations, painted by women as part of festival and marriage ceremonies, until as a result of a famine in the 1960s, they were painted on paper, to be sold as a means of raising desperately needed money.*

94 *A glass painting of Rama and Sita worshipping the* lingam. *Images such as this, painted in Thanjavur, Tamil Nadu, were once common devotional items in houses all over south India.*

95 ABOVE LEFT *A detail from a scroll depicting scenes from the* Ramayana, *used by itinerant performers from Midnapore, West Bengal. This scroll was painted by the performer's mother. It portrays the vulture Jatayu, the king of the birds, trying to rescue the abducted Sita from the clutches of Ravana, the demon-king of Lanka.*

96 ABOVE *A pata cloth painting of the bloodthirsty goddess Kali striding over the prone body of Shiva, from Raghurajpur, Orissa.*

97 This painted wooden model truck is from Rajasthan, although Trivandrum in Kerala is the traditional centre for this craft.

98 A cloth painting of Jagannath, Balabhadra and Subhadra in their temple at Puri, from either Puri or Raghurajpur. It is painted in a style that has remained unchanged for centuries.

99–101 OPPOSITE A selection of circular ganjifa playing cards, which are painted on cloth. Once cards of this type were made throughout India; nowadays Raghurajpur in Orissa is the only thriving centre of manufacture (TOP); A painted papier-mâché figure of Hanuman, the monkey chieftain, from Madhubani, Bihar (BOTTOM); A terracotta plaque painted in bright poster colours, from Molela, south Rajasthan. It depicts the folk deity Dharamraj (RIGHT).

102 A Warli mural painted in rice paste on a mud wall, depicting scenes from both the festivities and the workaday tasks of village life. The Warlis are tribal cultivators in the Thane district of north Maharashtra whose traditional art-forms were in the past restricted to images of the mother-goddess, but who have since the 1960s been encouraged to paint in a much freer narrative style.

103 It is the common practice amongst the Rathwa Bhils of Madhya Pradesh and eastern Gujarat to install a deity in the form of a ritual wall painting within the home. Outside the sacred enclosure other paintings, such as this, depict incidents from daily life, usually featuring horses.

104 *A wall painting in the forecourt*
of a haveli *(mansion) in Churi Ajitgarh,*
Jhunjhunu district, Rajasthan, portraying
rich local merchants going for a drive in
a 1930s British motor car.

105 ABOVE *A painting of Ganesh and his wives. Gouache on paper, Madhubani, Bihar.*

106 RIGHT *A pen-and-ink drawing of Matsya, the fish avatar of Vishnu, from Madhubani, Bihar.*

126

107 LEFT *Krishna and Radha, etched on palm leaf with an iron pen, the outline rubbed with lampblack, from Cuttack district, Orissa.*

108 RIGHT *A painting of Krishna and Radha on ivory, from Jaipur, Rajasthan.*

CHAPTER VII

A CRAFT MISCELLANY

There are many other crafts besides those based on such major material resources as wood or stone, or those definable as textiles or jewelry; some only employ a handful of people while others are of primary importance throughout the country. Amongst the latter are those that use leather and bamboo, which support massive crafts industries. Some have risen with new mass-produced manufactured products, particularly plastics, or have integrated these materials into traditional craftwork.

LEATHER

The leather industry is in the hands of some of the most ostracized of Hindu castes, who process dead animals, take the skin for leather, bones for glue and fresh meat for their own use. The Chamars buy and tan the leather and Mochis manufacture shoes, belts, harnesses and bags from it. So frowned upon is this processing of animal corpses that even the mechanized leather industries such as that of Kanpur are largely staffed by these communities.

The main product of the leather industry is footwear. In most north-Indian villages there will be a Mochi capable of making the coarse, tough slippers of thick buffalo or bullock hide that are worn by the peasantry. The sole consists of four or five layers of leather, in between two of which the cobbler sets out thin off-cuts, claiming that this increases the strength of the sole. He stitches along its axis using leather thongs or heavy thread, before sewing on the upper around the margin of the sole. Characteristically, village shoes have a long toe, which is turned back and stitched down onto the front of the upper.

The same craftsman would also make slippers for the middle-classes – shopkeepers, priests, teachers – that are much like Western slippers. Even smarter shoes are made that are often very ornate, since in many parts of the country the cobbler's womenfolk will decorate the slippers with stitchwork in brass or silver thread, either as part of a local craft or to order. An important centre for colourful embroidered shoes is around Bhinmal in southern Rajasthan, where the work is shared between men and women. Bhinmal slippers are now widely available in Rajasthan as well as in neighbouring states, and have become a popular tourist item.

In the warmer climes and seasons the preferred footwear is the *chappal* (sandal), which can be of a multitude of designs ranging from a simple sole, with a band running over the foot attached to a thong that passes between the big and second toes, to the tough Peshawari model – a solid, thick-soled, buckled sandal used originally by the tribesmen of the North-West Frontier to traverse a trackless

109 LEFT Kathputli *string puppets hanging outside a shop in Jaipur.*

rocky landscape. There are also all sorts of variations, factory-made in plastics and handmade from old tyres as well as leather. Most famous of all the Indian *chappals* are those made in Kolhapur district, in south-west Maharashtra. Here, the industry employs nearly five thousand households, most of these working at home in their villages to supply merchants in the city. Although the design and intricacy of the workmanship varies, the basic model has a thin sole, with a broad band running over the foot and a smaller one around the big toe, and two thongs that run between the toes joining the main band to the sole. All of these are made from embellished leather, although the complexity of the decoration will vary, and may include cut motifs, stitchwork, or areas of woven leather, whilst the thongs are usually plaited. Although the sole is thin, it is tough, made up of several layers, some with thin off-cuts inserted in between. It is said that this not only reinforces the sole but also makes the squeaking noise that is the hallmark of new, good-quality Kolhapuri *chappals*. The craftsmen say that their best sandals will withstand two years' constant use. The *chappals* are often kept the natural colour of the leather – a light tan – but some are dyed, most commonly being darkened with diesel oil.

The success of this industry inspired the cobblers of Athani, 100 kilometres (62 miles) east of Kolhapur in Karnataka state, to launch their own *chappal*-making enterprise, creating a rival centre, with the support of the state government. The Kolhapuris are scathing of their product, which they consider merely poor-quality copies (they maintain that the off-cuts between the layers of sole are made of cardboard as one of several ways of reducing costs).

European-style shoes are preferred by India's urban population and the younger rural folk for formal occasions such as weddings. These are largely factory-made, most importantly at Kanpur in Uttar Pradesh. Here the British founded a factory in the mid-19th century for the production of harnesses, saddles and belts for the Indian army. This concentrated tanning and leather work in the city, and the workers adapted to the changing demand. Many household units together produce cheap, Western-style footwear using traditional cobbling techniques aided by modern equipment, such as lethally unprotected bandsaws. Kanpur remains a major source of tanned and processed leather, supplying a large percentage of the leather-based industries – for example the coarse leather for ordinary slipper manufacture in Rajasthan is locally produced but the leather for the finer variety comes from Kanpur.

In a city like Hyderabad, in the Deccan, with its large Muslim population, special money belts are made for those going on the Haj pilgrimage to Mecca. These Haj belts fold double and are divided into a number of zipped, buttoned and even lockable pockets.

A small scattered craft dedicates itself to the making of leather puppets. These are produced in the ghats inland from the Karnataka coast, around Palghat (Kerala), and Nellore and Nimulkunta in Andhra Pradesh, where shadow puppets are a speciality. As with all rural entertainments, puppetry has suffered from the coming of film and television. Few puppets are made for professional performers; instead they have become toys and decorative items.

Before the advent of plastics, fluids were often transported in leather. The *bhisti* (water-carrier) with his water-bag made of whole goatskin can still occasionally be seen serving his customers. Camel caravans carried cooking oil and ghee in

large leather vessels, often made from the inner layer of camel skin. A branch of the Muslim Usta caste in Bikaner used to specialize in these vessels; they continue to make small oil bottles, flasks and jewel boxes from camel hide, which they decorate with painted designs. At Jaisalmer, camel-hide bottles with interesting carved wooden stoppers are made.

IVORY

Ivory-carving is an ancient Indian craft. The cluster of skeletons discovered around two tusks in excavations at Mohenjo-Daro were surely those of ivory-workers attempting to escape the destruction of their city with the raw materials of their craft. Ivory objects were also found in several of the Indus Valley settlements. Later, ivory is known to have become an important item of trade with the Roman empire. An inscription on a beautifully carved frieze at Sanchi, in Madhya Pradesh, records that it was presented and presumably worked by the ivory-carvers of the nearby town of Vidisa (2nd century AD).

In the recent past the craft was based in Kerala, Karnataka, especially in the coastal region, Pali and Jaipur (Rajasthan), Agra, Lucknow and Varanasi (Uttar Pradesh), Ahmedabad (Gujarat), and Behrampore and Murshidabad (West Bengal), in Orissa and in Delhi. There were many other subsidiary centres. The trade depended largely on imported African ivory, but the supply was gradually blocked off as African states began to ban export to conserve the elephant population. This was followed more recently by an international ban on the trade, bringing the craft to a virtual standstill (although some is still smuggled in). Craftsmen still rework old ivory, and there has been an attempt to substitute the natural material with 'semi-ivory' – a form of white acrylic to which powdered ivory is added to achieve a yellowing effect. This is worked into bangles and earrings with the same techniques as were used for pure ivory.

The demand was for functional items, especially combs, which were often richly decorated, fans, paper-knives, hairpins, buttons, and religious figures, particularly Hindu deities but also angels and saints for the Christian market (a craft developed by the Portuguese, mainly in Goa, during the 16th century). Other articles included pieces for chess, draughts, *chaupad* and for inlay-work in furniture, jewel boxes and musical instruments. In addition to carving figures in pure 'white' ivory, Rajasthani craftsmen also made the carving of cracked or inferior-grade ivory a speciality, painting it bright colours. Ivory craftsmen used to work with a selection of tiny chisels, using a bow lathe for the round objects such as the bangles. When the supply of ivory finally dried up, most of the craftsmen turned to related crafts such as sandalwood-, horn- or bone-carving, bringing to it the painstakingly detailed work that was traditional in ivory-carving.

TORTOISESHELL

Another craft that has been hard-hit by conservationist legislation is the working of tortoiseshell. As its breeding beaches have been invaded by man's developments and his ever-finer nylon fishing nets kill more each year, the turtle has become a threatened animal. Most Hindu fishermen will not kill them, since they consider them sacred, but once they have drowned in the nets, they can be turned to use. Of the many species of turtle, only two produce proper tortoiseshell, which occurs as thirteen thin plates on the carapace. The two small centres of tortoiseshell work in

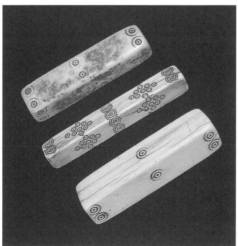

A painted leather oil bottle with a carved wooden stopper from western Rajasthan (top) and carved ivory dice, from Gujarat.

India are Visakhapatnam (Andhra Pradesh) and Diu, an island just off the Gujarat coast. In Visakhapatnam the shell was usually worked with ivory into fine jewelry boxes, and was rarely used by itself. The high cost, coupled with legislation banning the killing of turtles or the export of tortoiseshell items, has reduced the craft workforce in Diu to that of four men and one woman. Southern fishermen supply them with the shells of turtles that have either been washed up dead or caught in their nets when they are fishing for sawfish. They produce earrings, bracelets, solid bangles and necklaces made up of tortoiseshell pieces linked with silver wire. The shell is bent into an appropriate shape by placing it briefly in boiling water, manipulating it whilst it is soft, then quickly immersing it in cold water. Bangles are cut into shape and smoothed on a bow lathe. The surface is then highly polished with a hand buff.

A carved buffalo-horn comb from Sarai Tarin, Uttar Pradesh. Inset with brass wire and plastic, this comb is designed to hold scented hair oil, hence the bone plugs at either end.

BONE

Although in plentiful supply, bone has never been a very popular material in India. In some parts of the Himalayan foothills it is carved into ornaments which are covered with magical Tantric motifs and used by the priesthood. It was once widely used for combs, but the appearance of cheap bright plastic substitutes destroyed the market. The disappearance of ivory has increased interest in the material, however, and some Kerala ivory-carvers have been experimenting with bone, making chessmen, intricate pendants, necklaces and even walking-sticks. In Orissa some of the tribal communities make combs as well as excellent figures known as *mithuna* (loving couples). The main concentrations of bone-working are in Sarai Tarin and Nagina, in Uttar Pradesh. In both these places, handles are carved for the cutlery which is produced in nearby Moradabad, although this trade, too, is threatened by improved plastics. The carvers here also produce buttons, necklaces, cases for cigarettes, pen holders, animal figurines and even small vases.

HORN

For those working buffalo horn the staple demand, as with bone, was for hand-cut combs. This demand has largely disappeared, and in order to compete with the prices of plastic combs, the craftsmen have tended to dispense with attractive decoration. To make a comb, the craftsman flattens the horn after putting it in boiling water to render it soft. He then cuts it so that it tapers either side from a central flat area. Using a little saw blade, he makes a series of cuts along one edge to produce the teeth, before turning the comb and repeating the procedure on the opposite edge. Again, as with bone-carving, Sarai Tarin and Nagina in Uttar Pradesh produce much of this work. Here Muslim craftsmen still manufacture more ornate combs, cutting grooves into the surface to receive an inlay decoration of brass wire. Some are made hollow so that scented oil can be poured into the cavity (closed by a bone peg at each end) to percolate out into the hair as it is combed. In Orissa, especially at Cuttack, combs may be inset with silver filigree, which is also used to enliven horn bangles and perfume phials, known as *ittar dani*. During the 19th century a local prince established a centre for the production of horn artefacts at Parlakhemundi (Orissa). Horn animals, figures, pipes and lampstands are still produced there. At Sarai Tarin, earrings, necklaces and hair-clips extend the repertoire.

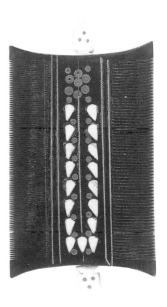

In Trivandrum, some ivory-carvers have turned to horn as a substitute material, often exploiting the curved natural form to make decorative items such as tigers, elephants or the ever-popular heron amidst the reeds. In West Bengal and Gujarat, brooches and bangles are produced. Small boxes in Ahmedabad and Surat are sometimes given a horn veneer.

To shape the horn, it is first made pliable by being kept moist in oil, then heated before a fire until it is almost as soft as wax. It is pressed into shape either by hand or with the help of a hardwood mould. Round pieces are finished on a bow lathe. In competition with plastics, the craft is in retreat; few young men want to follow their fathers into the craft and erstwhile centres of horn craftwork such as Honowar in Karnataka are now defunct.

SEA SHELLS

Shells are collected for many purposes. In Bengal, mother-of-pearl was collected for various craft items, especially trinkets such as bangles. In recent years a large industry has grown up in the south with Madras as its main centre. Here decorative hangings, mobiles, lampshades and screens are made from small shells pierced and threaded onto strings. Large cowries are incised with designs, pictures and greetings using the scraperboard technique to expose the white calcium beneath a mauve outer surface. A few families glue together combinations of shells, exploiting their natural form to produce human figures, animals and birds which are similar to those on sale at European seaside resorts.

SHOLA PITH

Pith taken from the stem of the shola (*Aeschynomene aspera*), a common water plant, is both light and a low heat conductor. The British exploited these properties by using it to make solar topis, the pith helmets that protected so many foreign heads from the lethal rays of the Indian sun. Fanny Parks, an observant memsahib writing in 1833, described a new craft producing more elaborate hats: 'At Meerut they cover them with the skin of the pelican, with all its feathers on, which renders it impervious to sun or rain, and the feathers sticking out beyond the rim of the hat give a demented air to the wearer.' That craft faded out with Independence, but the plant is still collected from nearby lakes; the straight stems, between 2 and 10 centimetres in diameter, can easily be peeled of their outer covering and the pith carved for decorative purposes.

In western Karnataka, women of the Gudigar caste make bridal garlands and coronets from it, decorating them with a multitude of little glass and golden 'jewels'. In West Bengal the Malakar community use pith to make bridal coronets and decorations for images of their deity, often in combination with paper pulp. They are particularly busy in the lead-up to great festivals, above all Durga Puja, when they must make a wonderful crown for the great goddess.

In Assam and Orissa many women still make pith decorations, but the most complicated and detailed work is done in Tamil Nadu. Here, artisans are renowned for their models of buildings, usually one of the great southern temples. Tiruchchirapalli, Madurai and to a lesser extent Thanjavur are particularly famous for their architectural models, each constructed from thousands of neatly worked fragments. The models are short-lived, since the organic nature of the material offers no protection against damage or decay.

FLOWERS

Perhaps the most ephemeral craft, however, but one nevertheless requiring considerable skill, is floral work. In much of India, marigolds, auspiciously saffron-coloured, are most popular for garlands and for the network of flowers that is draped over a car in preparation for a wedding. The south excels in fresh-flower work, and many thousands of men, women and children are involved in the trade. Garlands are carried to temples, draped around the neck of a guest or a notable, hung over holy pictures or parts of a vehicle to keep it safe, or over the portrait of a deceased relative. In the more intricate work, pictures or patterns are made up from various coloured petals. In the heat of that climate all are doomed to fade within a day.

BASKETRY AND MATS

In the manufacture of baskets, bamboo and to a lesser extent rattan are the principal materials used all over India. The bamboo is split into the required widths with a sharp knife, then the pieces are woven together, usually with the warps radiating out from a central base.

Some basket-makers are itinerants who buy their raw materials and then sit with their families on a piece of wasteground plaiting their baskets. They also make fans, winnowing trays and mats, all everyday necessities in rural India. Stools shaped like giant egg-timers, known as *moorah*, are made out of reeds and other materials all over north India. They will often supplement their range of wares with crude toys they make themselves, and with rattan furniture from south and north-east India.

The shapes of baskets vary with their function and the terrain over which they are to be carried. The baskets of the plains are in general wider than they are deep, with a low centre of gravity, and are designed to be carried on the head. For those peoples living in the hills, on the other hand, the most practical basket is deep, often conical, and carried on the back by means of arm straps or more usually a head strap. Baskets are made with a close weave or an open weave depending on their use: open-weave baskets, for example, are useful for carrying vegetables or other produce to market. The region comprising Assam and north-eastern India, with its abundant rain forests and stands of bamboo and rattan, has the most prolific and varied range of basketry in the subcontinent. Bamboo has many uses among the tribes of the north-east. Plates and baskets are fashioned from it, as are pipes and mugs. It also features widely in the construction of buildings and bridges. Open-work bamboo is used for making cattle muzzles in Assam and Tripura, and the special pig-carrying baskets of the Khasi people of Meghalaya. As elsewhere in India, bamboo is fabricated into winnowing fans and trays, and baskets to store and carry rice and other grains. Bamboo fish-traps of noteworthy ingenuity can be found in all the riverine and coastal districts of the subcontinent.

Baskets made of willow are a speciality of Kashmir. Based on English willow-work, they employ about two thousand people who produce basket, picnic and tiffin boxes in many different designs. The craft is relatively new, as a bush type of wicker willow was only introduced into Kashmir at the beginning of this century. Willow has certain advantages over both cane and bamboo in that it is stronger and less susceptible to insect damage. Srinagar and Hazratbal are the most important willow-work centres.

An Orissan woman plaiting a basket for vegetables from freshly cut and stripped bamboo.

In Bihar women make baskets and festival figures out of tough *sikki* grass. This is dyed brilliant colours before being plaited into basket form. This important craft is centred on the Mithila region of north Bihar.

In areas of heavy rainfall such as the north-east, Bengal, Orissa and the south, rain hats, umbrellas and rain capes are a necessity, and can also provide shelter from the harsh sun. Most of the hats are made by sandwiching a layer of dried leaves between two layers of a bamboo net-like structure. The 'country-made' umbrellas and rain capes follow similar principles of construction.

Rattans are the long slender stems of certain climbing palms which are mainly of the genus *Calamus*. Thirty species occur in India, mainly in the north-east and the tropical south. They are stripped, dried and used extensively for tying and binding, and for basketry and furniture. A speciality of Bengal and the north-east are coiled cane baskets, where the rattan canes are coiled up in a tight spiral. If the canes are of a softer variety, they are nailed together with bamboo splints; if harder, consecutive rows of the coiled cane are bound with split cane. Rattan cane furniture is an important industry in the north-east and the tropical south. A colonial innovation, it turns out chairs, tables, armchairs and other Western furnishing items. Blow-lamps are used to heat the cane before it can be bent to the required shape. The pre-shaped parts are then fixed into place with nails, the joints bound with split cane and the hard silica-containing outer layer of the rattan scraped off – this both reveals the inner surface and gets rid of the burn marks from the blow-torch.

A variety of grasses and to some extent palm leaves are the primary material for most of the mats made in India. The *madur* mats of West Bengal are woven from the thin soft *madur kathi* reed cultivated in Midnapore district. Dyed *kora* grass is used to make the beautiful mats of Pathamadai, Tirunelveli district (Tamil Nadu), and in its undyed state it is plied into the golden *korai* mats of Orissa. In Kerala they often mix *kora* grass with the leaves of the screwpine in very pleasing combinations. Leaves of the date and the palmyra palms are also used in many parts of India. Finest of all, however, are the *sitalpatti* mats of Bengal, Assam and Tripura, for which *mutra* cane is soaked and then split into thin strips before it is woven into these extremely fine and flexible mats. Women weave these mats on a bamboo- or timber-frame loom. Cotton string is generally used for the warps.

A sikki-*grass basket depicting Krishna and Radha, made in Bihar.*

MUSICAL INSTRUMENTS

India has a great history of classical music that stretches back to the days of the Vedas. North and south India have very different musical traditions, however, and often radically different instruments. The folk base from which India's classical music tradition springs is still much in evidence: it may be the village potter come to beat his *dholak* drum for a village wedding; a shepherd playing his bamboo flute to his flock; or pious women singing *bhajan* (hymns) in praise of Lord Krishna, to the accompaniment of *kartal* rattles and a harmonium.

Playing the sitar, the *veena*, tablas and a gamut of string, wind and percussion instruments that theoretically could number more than five hundred, India's classical musicians give concerts in great halls and recitals for select gatherings sponsored by rich industrialists, and make recordings and broadcasts.

Some instruments are made and used at village level. To make a bamboo flute or a simple *jantra* may require skill but does not presuppose any sophisticated technology. Such instruments as the *banam* of the Santhal tribals of West Bengal and Bihar, with its neck carved in anthropomorphic shapes, are also virtually home-made.

Professional musicians, however, require professionally made instruments. The great instrument-making centres in north India are Calcutta, Uttar Pradesh (especially Lucknow and Varanasi) and Delhi. The primary centres for south-Indian instruments are Miraj in Maharashtra, Thanjavur in Tamil Nadu, Hyderabad, Madras and Mysore. Miraj and Thanjavur are particularly notable for their making of *tamburas*. Nearly all instruments are produced in small workshops, which either specialize in a certain type or produce a whole range of high-quality instruments that are custom-made. In the Lal bazaar area of Calcutta, craftsmen can be seen at work producing sitars, sarods, violins and tablas. Western-style drums, guitars and brass instruments are also made. All are small-scale industries. The workshops employ between five and forty men, many of whose antecedents have been craftsmen in this industry for generations.

Materials used in instrument manufacture are both indigenous and imported. Local toon and teak wood are used to make the neck of a sitar, while the bowl is fashioned from a gourd. Pegs are made from rosewood, the bridge from stagshorn and the inlay would once have been made of ivory. The frets are of locally made base metal and the strings are of steel or phosphorous bronze imported from England. Tablas will be made from *margosa* or *shisham* wood, with goat leather for the adjusting straps. The accompanying *bayan* drum may be of brass or copper, but the best ones are clay.

All the instrument-makers complain about the lack of government help or crafts award structure which, given the international prominence of Indian music, is indeed perplexing. Costs for the instrument-makers are considerable. Wood is dear and requires years of seasoning. The best makers first have to train their apprentices as musicians so that they can tune the instruments, after which they are in great danger of losing them before they can recoup the expense of their training. But despite these problems, it is a healthy industry with a strong local and export market, and with the continued popularity of Indian music, looks set to remain so.

Some of these crafts are doomed, especially when their primary raw materials – such as ivory and tortoiseshell – are no longer easy to come by, and some have totally disappeared in the face of cheaper substitutes. Many people were employed until the late 19th century in catching brightly coloured beetles and removing and drying their wing cases as decorative items. The beetles have been saved by cheap, mass-produced decorations such as sequins. The indomitable Fanny Parks, writing in 1826, mentions the craft: 'Beetle wings are procurable at Benares, and are used there for ornamenting *kimkhwab* and native dresses. In Calcutta and Madras, they embroider gowns for European ladies with these wings, edged with gold; the effect is beautiful.' Poona was another centre for this extinct industry and one can still come across articles – from clothing to camel harnesses – that bear these bright green, jangling fragments. Other crafts such as shoe and basket manufacture, fuelled by rich sustainable resources and healthy demand, promise to flourish for many decades; but all crafts live under threat, and the world will be a poorer place for their passing.

A Kashmiri musician playing a sarod inlaid with mother-of-pearl.

110 RIGHT *A goat-skin puppet of Ravana, the evil, ten-headed king of Lanka. Painted with vegetable pigments, these puppets are made in western Andhra Pradesh by a community that has migrated from Maharashtra.*

111 *Sikki grass bowls such as this are made in many places in Bihar state.*

112 *A circular fan made from fine bamboo splints, from Nalchar village near Agartala, Tripura.*

113 RIGHT *A storage basket for clothes from Manipur, known as a* phingaruk. *It comprises a container and semi-spherical lid, both of woven bamboo.*

114 *An articulated toy crocodile made of shola pith, from Assam.*

115 *A pandanus palm-leaf baby's rattle, from Tamil Nadu.*

116 RIGHT *A painted mythological figure made of shola pith, from Assam.*

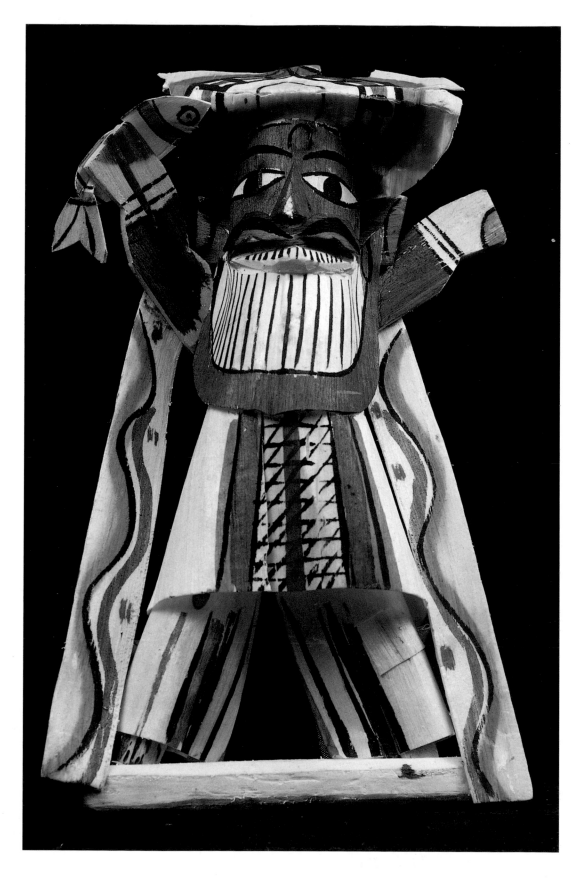

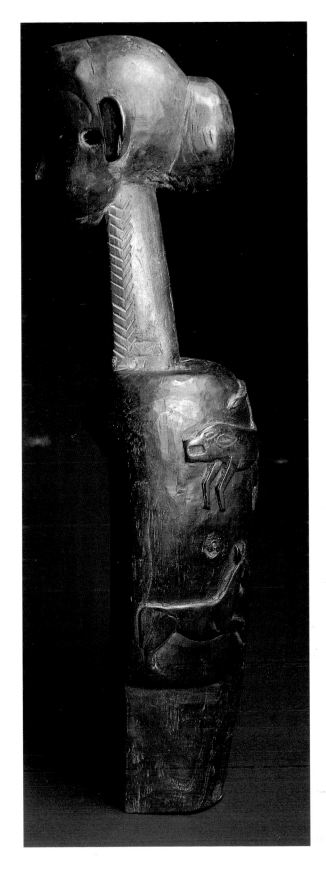
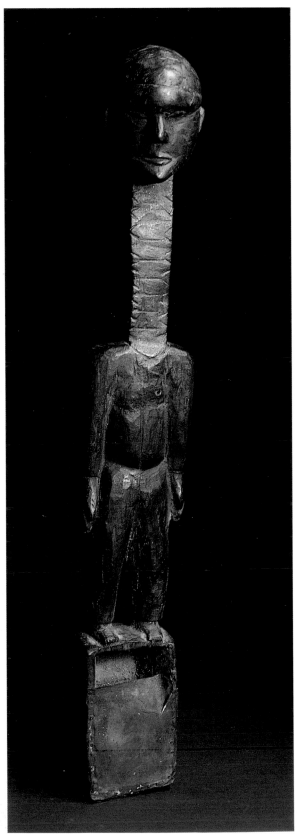

117, 118 LEFT Banam – *carved wooden stringed instruments given human shape – made by Santhal tribesmen from Bihar.*

119 RIGHT *The tambura is a drone instrument which utilizes a large gourd covered with a thin plate of rosewood as a resonator. The bridge is of stag's horn, the decorative inlay of ivory and the pegs of teak. This instrument was made at Varanasi.*

120, 121 LEFT *Elephants painted for a festival in Rajasthan. The forehead and upper trunk are decorated with auspicious designs.*

122 BELOW *A woman stringing garlands of marigold flowers by the roadside outside Jaipur.*

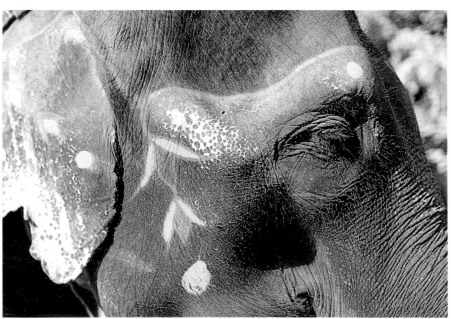

123 *A garland adorning a wayside shrine in Jaipur.*

Within Jaipur's City Palace four doorways, each named after a Hindu season, give onto the Pritam Niwas Courtyard. They are adorned with stucco relief figures and spectacular painted motifs, often imitating tilework. Above each door is an appropriate marble deity.

124 ABOVE *Running into the shade of the cusped arch recess is a lotus-petal motif, which radiates from the lintel of the door.*

125 RIGHT *On the Peacock Gate, painted stucco peacocks in high relief surround the marble figure of a deity. Around it a nimbus of lotus petals merges into the chevron motif once favoured for cloth screens.*

126 ABOVE *Ganesh, attended by his consorts Riddhi and Siddhi, sits framed in a stucco arch. As lord of beginnings, he is the most common figure to preside over a lintel. Such carved deities are still turned out in large numbers by craftsmen based in the south-west sector of walled Jaipur.*

127 RIGHT *The Peacock Gate, most famous of the four, symbolizes the rainy season. Peacocks and turbaned figures moulded in stucco relief guard the entrance to the palace. Jaipur's stucco and painted wall decorations were once widely famous. The motifs were constructed either on a series of compass arcs and lines or on stencilled outlines.*

128–30 Hammered out against a die, the relief portrayal of a diseased part of the body is presented to the deity in the hope of a cure. These silver hands, ears and eye have been made for this purpose at Nasik, Maharashtra, a major centre of pilgrimage.

131 RIGHT A cast brass effigy of a Shaivite figure, from Belgaum district, Karnataka.

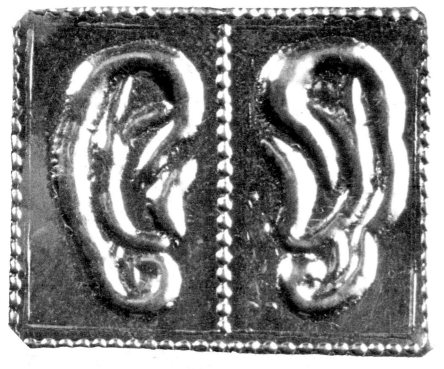

132 LEFT *Floral wall panels such as this Jaipur mural reached their peak in early 17th-century Mughal buildings. The fashion then spread to the Rajput courts of Rajasthan. The plant was first sketched on paper, then its outline pierced with a stylus to create a stencil. This was pounced over with a cloth bag of soot, transferring a dotted outline onto the plaster.*

133 RIGHT *A lotus design from a Jaipur mural. The lotus is sacred to the Hindus, and is particularly popular in decorative art, full use being made of the curve of the stem, positioning of the leaves and tilt of the blooms to produce a rich pattern.*

COLLECTING INDIAN ARTS AND CRAFTS

To many people, collecting is half the joy of travel. To wander through the market-place, stop and then haggle gently over the price of some object that catches the eye can often teach you much about the people and their culture. The whole of India is akin to some great bazaar, as the sub-continent has from ancient times lived by trade. It was always one of the world's most important commercial cross-routes, its people one of the great merchant communities of Asia.

Everywhere in India there is the temptation to buy, and always a clever salesman to help you succumb. For tourists, the main points of entry into India are Delhi and Bombay airports. To the capital come all the crafts of the north and a great deal from the rest of the country. Jan Path, the main shopping street of New Delhi, is the place to start. The Tibetan market outside the Imperial Hotel has a wide selection of curios.

Further towards Connaught Place, Gujarati women sell embroidery. Antiques can be bought inside the Red Fort in Old Delhi and at Sunder Nagar market. The most comprehensive selection of craft goods can be found at the Central Cottage Industries emporium on Janpathat, and the state government emporia on Baba Kharak Singh Marg. Each state has a retail outlet on this road, and some of the more important states have emporia in other major cities.

Bombay is the commercial capital of India, the vibrant hub of the nation's business. There is a maze of antique shops behind the Taj Mahal Hotel in Colaba, where pavement-sellers also congregate, displaying their textiles and other crafts. The Chor ('thieves') bazaar and the Bindi bazaar are the places to find old brass and other second-hand goods. In Calcutta the craft shops and curio emporia are located on Chowringee by the Grand Hotel and in the New Market area.

Major craft-producing states such as Gujarat, Rajasthan, Uttar Pradesh, Andhra Pradesh and Orissa have specific towns, cities or regions that are most worth visiting. In Gujarat it is Ahmedabad (Law Gardens and Ashram Road) and Kutch; in Rajasthan, Udaipur, Jodhpur and above all Jaipur; in Uttar Pradesh, Varanasi and in Andhra Pradesh, Hyderabad. In Orissa the best place is the temple town of Puri. The wares of Kashmir, of course, are found in Srinagar, its capital. In the south, sales are concentrated in Madras, Bangalore, and in the intriguing Synagogue Street in Cochin.

As far as textiles are concerned, cotton, silk and woollen embroideries, weavings and carpets are to be found in abundance. They have the advantage of usually being modestly priced, light, and easy to pack and transport home without fear of damage. The most important tourist regions, such as Rajasthan, Kashmir, parts of the Himalayas, Goa and Kerala, are either situated close to, or are themselves, major textile-producing areas. Both commercial and traditional Gujarati embroidery can now be found all over India at much the same price, as can Kashmiri embroidery and carpets, although in both cases the home state offers the greatest variety, as well as an increased chance of finding something special. Block-printed cotton bedspreads and yardage are produced in many states, but Rajasthan has the greatest range, and good examples can be picked up cheaply in any town. Vivid tie-dye can be bought in the bazaars of Jodhpur and Jaipur, but the best work is from Kutch. Cotton ikat is produced commercially in Orissa and Andhra Pradesh, and is best bought there, or else in the government emporia. (The word ikat is not generally known in India. You will have a better chance of being understood if you use the word *patola*, although strictly this applies to silk double-ikat from Gujarat.) If you are looking for cotton wraps or sarongs, for the beach or for nightwear, the obvious choice are the beautifully woven, cool Madras checks from Tamil Nadu, or its vivid batik, also made in Kerala. Woollen shawls come from Kashmir or the Kulu valley, but are widely available throughout India. Silk saris or yardage originate mainly from Varanasi and Assam in the north, and from Bangalore and Kanchipuram in the south, but can be bought in shops and emporia all over the subcontinent. One of the best sources of silk saris is the Kala Mandir chain of shops.

Jewelry, of course, is also easily transportable. Jaipur and the silver bazaar off Chandni Chowk in Old Delhi are both accessible centres of jewelry manufacture. Prices for precious metals, silver and gold are set daily, and the current rate per gram can be found in a daily paper. Indian silver prices are marginally higher than world rates, and gold prices are often markedly so. Most jewelry is sold by weight, at the current market price, although one often has to pay a premium per gram when buying antique jewelry, which has to be negotiated. The piece will be weighed on accurate scales before your eyes, but the purity of the metal is often a matter of dispute, as there is no system of hallmarking, and customers have only their judgment and experience to rely on (although it is possible – but extremely time-consuming – to get pieces assayed). Buying a simple silver piece is relatively easy; the problems come with hollow pieces filled with shellac or necklaces strung with glass and other beads as well as precious metal.

Do you pay the precious-metal price for the whole object or just a percentage of it, and if so what percentage? Ulltimately, decisions are usually made on aesthetic grounds, while taking into account the precious-metal content, standard of workmanship and design.

Most towns in India have a jewelry bazaar. Older pieces are generally better crafted, but these are not necessarily on display. It is always a good idea to ask the jewelry-seller whether he has any old silver, and he may well extract some interesting items from his drawer. Bhuj (Kutch), and towns and cities in Rajasthan, Kashmir and Orissa are good places to buy silver, while Hyderabad is world-famous for its cultured pearls, but the best worked gold is often found in the south. The centre of the semi-precious stone trade is Jaipur.

Paintings on cloth, paper and even ivory are best purchased in Rajasthan, particularly in Jaipur, and in Orissa. Most papier-mâché products come from the Kashmir valley, but can be bought all over India. The most interesting basketry is found in Assam and Bihar, and the best patterned matting is made in Tamil Nadu and Assam.

Carved and painted wood can be found all over India, but primarily in Gujarat, Rajasthan, Kashmir, Tamil Nadu and Karnataka, famous for its sandalwood carving. Lacquered wood comes from Rajasthan, Gujarat and Kerala.

Moradabad in Uttar Pradesh is by far the most prolific centre of brass production, although Moradabad brassware can be bought all over India and at many other places throughout the world. *Dokla* (lost-wax figures) are made in the tribal belt that runs through Bengal, Bihar, Orissa and Andhra Pradesh, and are best bought in the state government emporia. Clay pots and figurines of animals or dolls are made all over the subcontinent, and are easy and cheap to buy, although fragile, and heavy to carry.

To put your purchases into their cultural context, visits to Indian museums can be very fruitful. The Crafts Museum in New Delhi (on Bhairon Marg, by the side of Purana Qila – the Old Fort) is an ideal place to start. Built up by successive curators as a labour of love, it not only houses a comprehensive collection of all manner of Indian crafts, but for most of the year also has rural artisans from different parts of India practising their craft in the museum yard. What they produce on site is for sale, and the museum shop always stocks interesting albeit sometimes quite expensive examples of their work. Another opportunity to see and buy craft is at the crafts *mela* (festival) that takes place every February at Suraj Kund, just outside Delhi on the Haryana border. The National Museum in New Delhi, the Indian Museum in Calcutta, the Prince of Wales Museum in Bombay and the Madras Museum are well worth a visit. For those interested in textiles the Calico Museum (Retreat, Shahi Bagh, Ahmedabad) is one of the most outstanding textile museums in the world. Of the smaller regional museums, the eclectic and sometimes eccentric Palace Museum at Bhuj, the capital of Kutch, is always a favourite.

Elsewhere in the world, such museums as the Victoria and Albert, and the Museum of Mankind (London), the Tropen Museum (Amsterdam), the Metropolitan Museum (New York), the Smithsonian (Washington), the M.H. de Young Museum (San Francisco), the U.C.L.A. Museum of Cultural History and the Museum of International Folk Art (Santa Fe) all have Indian collections of great interest as well as comprehensively stocked bookshops. If you happen to acquire something out of the ordinary, most of these museums will be happy to identify it for you if approached through the proper channels.

Great Britain is the most abundant source of Indian crafts outside India, owing in equal measure to the close historical links between the countries and the post-Independence migration of many communities from the subcontinent. Antique shops and markets all over the country, but most particularly in London, are a wonderful source of old Indian craft artefacts. It is much easier to find some items, such as old *jamawar* shawls from Kashmir, in London than it is in New Delhi. London also has a thriving wholesale market for much modern Indian craft, which is disseminated all over the country and exported to the rest of Europe. The mainly Punjabi district of Southall is the centre of this wholesale trade. In the rest of Europe, the major towns and cities of Spain, France, the Netherlands, Switzerland, Italy and Germany will all have some kind of Indian craft shop.

The great wealth and cosmopolitan population of North America has attracted goods from all over the world. New York, Los Angeles, San Francisco, Boston, Toronto and Montreal all have excellent Indian craft shops, and there is a concentration of exquisite examples to be found in New Mexico. Tokyo also has fine Indian craft goods; Indian textiles, in particular, appeal to Japanese sensibility.

The areas of the world with which India has a long trading history, such as South-East Asia, the East African littoral, the Persian Gulf and the Arabian peninsula – indeed, the whole of the Middle East – are littered with Indian craft items, both new and old. Curiously, the owners of tourist shops from such diverse places as Jerusalem and Marrakesh will come to India for handicrafts to pad out their native stock, which is surely a richly deserved accolade and tribute to the quality and diversity of India's hand-crafted products.

PLACES TO BUY INDIAN ARTS AND CRAFTS

Australia
Sydney India, 92 Oxford St., Paddington, Sydney, 02021 N.S.W.

Belgium
Antwerp Coppens Tribal Art, Grote Peperstraat 69, 2700 Sint-Nicklaas; De Witte Uil, Kammenstraat 14–16, 2000 Antwerp
Brussels Kalou, 49 rue de la Fauvette, 1180 Brussels

Canada
Montreal Woven Gardens, 451 Sherborne St. West, Montreal H3G 2W4
Toronto Frida Crafts, 39 Front St. East, Ontario M5E 1B3; Vernacular, 1130 Yonge St., Ontario M4W 2L8

France
Paris Haga, 22 rue de Grenelle, 75007 Paris

Germany
Braunschweig Banana, Handelsweg 11, 33 Braunschweig
Cologne Lothar Heubel, Breitestrasse 118-120, 50667 Cologne
Dusseldorf Raritaten-Raek, Hahnenfurtherstrasse 3, 40629 Dusseldorf
Ennepetal Kayu, Freidenshohe 11, 58256 Ennepetal
Munich Galerie Mashallah, Schellingstrasse 52, 8000 Munich 40
Hamm Goa, Oststrasse 13, 59065 Hamm
Stuttgart Koken, Esslingerstrasse 14, 7000 Stuttgart

Great Britain
Belfast Dennis Cope, 16 Locksley Gardens, Belfast BT10 OAE
Berkhampstead Sanuk, Little Heath Farm, Potton End, Berkhampstead
Brighton Ananda, 19 Bond St., Brighton BN1 4AL
Cambridge John Gillow, 50 Gwydir St., Cambridge CB1 2LL; Nomads, Kings Parade, Cambridge CB2 1FJ; Rosie MacMurrray, Market Place, Cambridge
Cirencester Cargo, 23 Market Place, Cirencester GL7 2NX
Edinburgh Galerie Mirage, 46a Raeburn Place, Edinburgh EH4 1HL; Rufus Reade, 40 Pilrig St., Edinburgh EH6 5AL
Exeter Chandni Chowk, 1 Harlequins, Exeter EX4 3TT
Haddenham Alastair Hull, The Old Mill, The Green, Haddenham, Cambridge CB6 3TA
Harrogate Ankh, 14 Prince's St., Harrogate HG1 1NH
Heswell Ethnique, 108 Telegraph Rd, Heswell, Merseyside
Knaresborough Gordon Reece Gallery, Finkle St., Knaresborough, HG5 8AA
Leamington Spa Mystique, 92 Regent St., Leamington Spa
London The Beagle Gallery, 303 Westbourne Grove W11 2QA; The Conran Shop, Michelin House, 81 Fulham Rd, SW3 6RD; Country and Eastern, 3 Holland St., W8 4NA; Dave Edmonds' Emporium, Arch 4, Antique Alley, Stables Market, Chalk Farm Road, NW1 6TP; David and Charles Wainwright, 251 Portobello Rd, W11 1LT; Dennis Woodman Gallery, 105 North Road, Kew, Surrey, TW9 4DJ; General Trading Co., 144 Sloane St., SW1X 9BL; Global Village, 247–9 Fulham Rd, SW3 6HY; India Works, 107a Pimlico Rd, SW1 8PH; Joss Graham Oriental Textiles, 10 Eccleston St, SW1W 9LT; Liberty's Basement, 210–20, Regent St., W1R 6AH; Lunn Antiques, 86 New Kings Road, SW6 4LU; Neal Street East, 5–7 Neal St., WC2H 9PU; Nice Irma's, 46 Goodge St., W1P 1FJ; Rau, 36 Islington Green, N1 8DU; Tessa Hughes, Denmark Lodge, Crescent Grove, SW4 7AG;
Ludlow Anthony Sheppard, 2 Castle St., Ludlow SY8 1AT
Lytham Worth's, The Coach House, Henry St., Lytham, Lancashire FY8 5LE
Marden Richard Lightbaum, Indigo, The Barn, Grange Farm, Marden, Wiltshire SN10 3RQ
Norwich Country and Eastern, 8 Redwell St, Norwich NR2 4SN
Petersfield Far Horizons, 16 Ram's Walk, Petersfield

Stockbridge Read-Molteno Gallery; Nomads' House, High St, Stockbridge
South Petherton Global Village, 17 St James St., South Petherton, Somerset TA13 5BS
Tetbury Art-Tique, 18 Long St, Tetbury, Gloucestershire GL8 8AQ
Wales Ian Snow, Wylfa, Carno, Powys

The Netherlands
Utrecht De Paradysvogel, Voorstraat 44, Utrecht

India
Ahmedabad Gujari, Ashram Rd
Bombay Bindi Bazaar; Chor Bazaar;
Calcutta Curio Emporium, Grand Hotel Chowringee
Cochin Synagogue St.
Jaipur Saurashtra Oriental Arts, Opp Ayuverda College
Hyderabad Andhra Pradesh Government Emporium, Gun Foundry
Madras Tamil Nadu Government Emporium, Mount Rd
New Delhi Cottage Industries Emporium, Jan Path; The State Emporia, Babakharak Singh Marg; The Crafts Museum Shop, Bhairon Marg, by the Old Fort; The Shopping Arcade, the Red Fort; Sunder Nagar Markct, Mathura Rd

Italy
Cagliari Fior di Loto, Via Satta No 27, 09127 Cagliari
Milan Etno Arte, Via Marsala No 1, 20121 Milan
Novara Samarcanda, Via dei Gantieri No 6, Novara
Venice Paropamiso, 1701 Via San Marco (Frizzeria), 30100 Venice

Japan
Tokyo Hiroko Iwatate, 25-13 Jiyugaoka-1, Meguroku, Tokyo-152

Portugal
Lisbon De Natura, 162A Rua de Rosa, 1200, Lisbon

Spain
Barcelona Puerto Galerra, Dr Roux, 30 Torre, Barcelona 17
Seville Caroline Stone, Santa Teresa 3; Seville 41004

Switzerland
Zurich Annapurna, Scheitergasse 10, 8001; Nomadenschatze, Kirchgasse, 8001

U.S.A.
Argyle Maharani, 132 Jester Rd, Argyle, Texas
Baltimore People United, 4109 Roland Avenue, Baltimore, MD 21211
Evanston Marketplace, Handiwork of India, 1461 Ashland Avenue, Evanston, IL 60201
Gainsville Alternatives of Gainsville, 1013 West University Avenue, Gainsville, FL 32601
New York The Antique and Decorative Textile Company, 254 West 73rd St., NY 10023; The Craft Barn, 30 Wheeler Rd, P.O. Box 577, Florida, NY 10921; Jacques Carcanagues, Inc. 106 Spring St., NY 10012; Leekan Designs, 93 Mercer Street, NY 100012; Nusraty Imports, 215 West 10th Street (corner Bleecker), NY 10014
San Diego Bazaar del Mundo, 2754 Calhoun Street
Santa Fe Origins, 135w, San Francisco St., S7 New Mexico
Seemanta, Box 9057, Santa Fe, New Mexico 87504
Trade & Travel Routes, Route 9, Box 53D, Santa Fe NM 87505
San Francisco Folk Art International, Gheradelli Square, 900 Northpoint, San Francisco 94109
Seattle Kandahar Trading Co. Inc., 1605 12th Avenue, Seattle, WA 98122
Wayzata Consecha Designs, 746 East Mill St., Wayzata, MN 55391

MAP

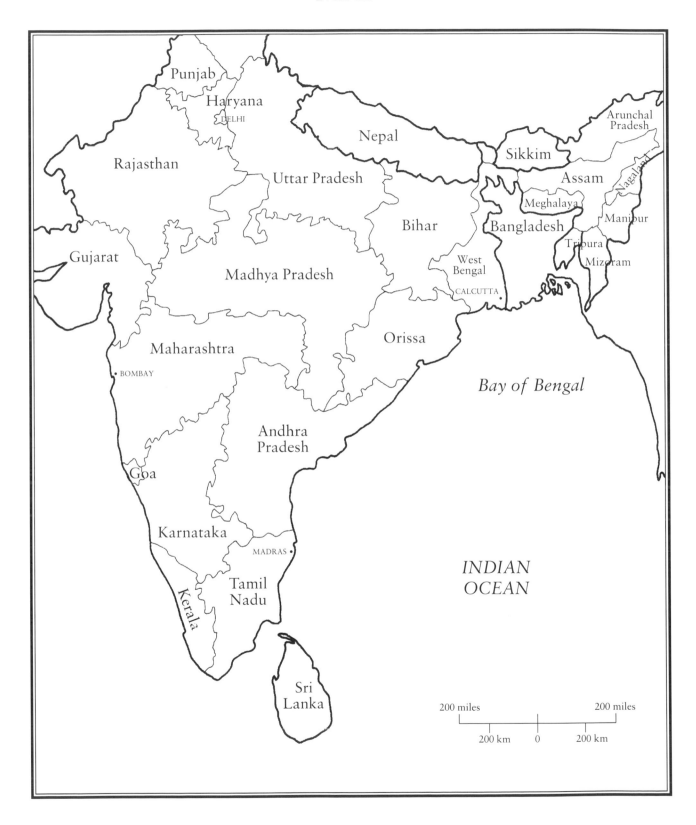

Punjab

Haryana

DELHI

Nepal

Arunchal
Pradesh

Sikkim

Rajasthan

Uttar Pradesh

Assam

Meghalaya

Nagaland

Manipur

Bihar

Bangladesh

Tripura

Gujarat

Madhya Pradesh

West
Bengal

Mizoram

CALCUTTA

Orissa

Maharashtra

Bay of Bengal

• BOMBAY

Andhra
Pradesh

Goa

INDIAN
OCEAN

Karnataka

MADRAS •

Kerala

Tamil
Nadu

Sri
Lanka

200 miles

200 miles

200 km

0

200 km

GLOSSARY

annealing The process whereby metal is heated and then cooled, to soften it, and hence avoid the risk of cracking consequent upon any cold working of the metal.

ajrarkh Cloth of predominantly indigo colouring, block-printed (usually on both sides) with geometric patterning, in Sind, western Rajasthan and Kutch.

batik A method for resist-dyeing cloth whereby a waxy substance is applied to selected areas, rendering them impervious to dye.

bandhani The Gujarati word for the resist technique of tie and dye.

Bania Member of the Hindu business caste with a reputation for money-lending.

Banjara This caste of north Indian origin, who once specialized in the transportation of goods, is now found in many places, particularly central India. Banjara women produce some of the most intricately stitched folk embroidery in all India.

bhagna J shaped blow-pipe used by Indian jewelers.

Bhil A tribal people found on marginal land, principally in north and east Gujarat, south-east Rajasthan and western Madhya Pradesh.

bhoota figures Temple effigies of carved jackwood, from around Udipi in Karnataka.

Bhuta A trader inhabiting the Himalayan valleys.

bidri A process of decoration whereby silver sheet and wire are inlayed into cast pieces of blackened zinc alloy. First practised at Bidar in Karnataka.

Brahmin The priestly caste of Hindus (Brahmins are not, however, restricted to the priesthood as an occupation; many stone-carvers, for instance, are Brahmin).

brazing A jointing technique similar to soldering whereby a brazing rod melts onto the joint under the heat of a torch.

champlevé A type of enamelling much practised in India, whereby the enameller gouges out troughs in the surface of the metal and fills them with enamel.

chandrahaar Marriage necklace of enamelled plaques and silver chains, from Himachal Pradesh.

chappal Indian sandal.

charpoy Ubiquitous wooden-framed, string-laced bed (lit. 'four feet').

chasing A finishing process involving the crisping-up of a repoussé design from the front with a hammer and punches.

chaupad Indian game (also known as *parcheesi*) played on a cross-shaped board or cloth, from which the English game of ludo is derived.

Chettiar A powerful Tamil merchant caste who became very wealthy as a result of the trade with South-East Asia.

cloisonné Method of enamelling whereby the surface of the object is built up with tiny walls to form the cells into which the enamel can be fused.

chillum Conical pipe – often terracotta – for smoking hashish or tobacco.

chintz World-renowned painted and printed textiles of great beauty and delicacy, once exported in great quantities to Europe from the Coromandel coast of south-east India.

chitrakar Painter.

Dassehra Hindu festival commemorating Rama setting off to rescue his wife Sita from the clutches of the demon-king Ravana.

Diwali Hindu festival of light.

doming block Metal cube or slab where a range of hemispherical recesses are cut.

Dravidians Pre-Aryan inhabitants of India, still forming the largest racial component in southern India.

draw plate A metal plate pierced with a series of tapering holes used for reducing or changing the cross-section of wire.

dhurrie Flatwoven cotton rug or coverlet.

enamelling The process of fusing differently coloured vitreous glazes to the surface of metal.

engraving The process of removing metal from the surface to create decoration or lettering with a sharp-edged tool.

filigree The technique of using silver or gold wire to build up items of jewelry or other ornaments.

ganjifa Circular Indian playing cards painted on layers of glued cloth. They come in sets of 96, 120 or 144 to accommodate 8, 10, or 12 different suits.

granulation Process whereby gold or silver granules (small spheres of metal) are set in patterns and joined to the surface by fusion welding.

Ghats Lines of hills rising from the coastal plains flanking the east and west of the Deccan plateau (also, steps leading down to a bathing-place).

Gond A tribal people found throughout central India.

Gudigar A caste of south Indian wood-carvers.

Haj The Muslim pilgrimage to Mecca.

Harappa One of the two most important cities of the Indus civilization to be excavated.

hasli A torque, usually of silver, popular with peasant and pastoralist women all over India.

Indo-Aryans Herding people, probably of Caucasian origin, speaking an Indo-European language, large numbers of whom invaded northern India in the second millennium BC.

ikat The resist-dyeing process in which designs are reserved into the warp or weft yarns by tying off small bundles of threads to prevent the penetration of dye.

Jain Follower of the religious teachings of

Mahavir, a contemporary of Gautama Buddha. Mahavir's teachings emphasized the concept of *ahimsa* – non-violence – and strict vegetarianism.

jali Pierced screen of stone, wood or wrought iron.

jamdani Fabric of fine cotton muslin woven in Bengal (and once also at Tanda and Varanasi, in Uttar Pradesh).

Jat Farming and herding caste found all over north India.

jhumka A type of earring incorporating pendant bell shapes, long fashionable with Muslims.

kabeez Propitiary figure of clay or other material.

kalamkari Hand-painted cloths of Masulipatnam and Kalahasti, Andhra Pradesh (much of the Masulipatnam production is in fact block-printed, but the cloths are still known as *kalamkaris*). Literally, 'penwork'.

kantha Cotton cover embroidered by the women of Bengal on quilted layers of old discarded *dhotis* or saris.

khadi Hand-woven cotton cloth.

kharkhanas Court craft workshops, particularly of the Mughals.

kinkhab Heavy silk brocaded fabric often incorporating real silver threads.

kulhar Disposable clay pot in which syrupy sweets are sold.

Khasi A tribal people found in Meghalaya and Assam.

leheria A resist-dyeing technique that results in multi-striped or chequered multi-coloured patterning.

Lohar Itinerant tinker and blacksmith community of north-west India.

Lost wax A casting process whereby a wax model of the required piece, having been surrounded by investment, is melted out, leaving a cavity into which the molten metal is forced. Also known as 'cire perdue'.

lota Small, pot-shaped vessel, usually made of brass.

lungi Man's unstitched sarong-like nether-garment.

mashru A warp-faced textile of mixed fabric, combining a silk (or now usually synthetic) warp and a cotton weft.

mordant A metallic salt that combines chemically with the dyestuff to fix the dye permanently.

makara Mythological beast.

Mali The gardener caste found in north India.

Manasa The snake goddess, worshipped particularly in Bengal.

masala A mixture of substances.

mangal sutra A marriage necklace of black gun-metal and gold beads, popular all over north and west India.

marquetry Inlay work of wood forming a decorative pattern on the surface of a wooden object.

Marwari   A member of a Rajasthani trading caste which is now the dominant force in business and industry throughout India.

maund   Indian measure of weight.

Mizo   Tribal people of north-east India.

mohalla   The sector of an Indian town occupied by a certain caste, religious or occupational group.

Mohenjo-Daro   One of the two most important cities of the Indus civilization.

Mughal   The ruling dynasty of India from 1526 to 1857.

Naga   A group of many tribes found in the hill tracts of north-east India and across the border into Burma.

naturapetty   Nine-sided decorative dowry-box from Kerala, usually of painted jackwood.

nau ratan   The nine astrologically auspicious gems, often worn for their protective qualities.

naqsha   Map, or pattern.

paambadam   Heavy gold earrings incorporating the shapes of six different styles of earrings amalgamated together, worn by rural women in Tamil Nadu.

Pahari   A style of miniature painting of the Rajput courts in what is now Himachal Pradesh (literally, 'of the hills').

palliya   Carved memorial stones found in rural Kutch and Saurashtra, and amongst the Bhils of eastern Gujarat.

Parsi   Zoroastrian descendant of refugees who fled from Persia in the 8th century after the Muslim invasion. Now sadly declining in population, they nevertheless count amongst their number some of India's most prominent industrialists.

patachitra   Cloth paintings of Jagannath and associated deities painted at Puri and other centres in Orissa.

patara   Massive brass-bound wooden bridal chest from Gujarat.

patola   Famous double-ikat silk saris now woven only at Patan, Gujarat, but once also at Surat and other towns.

perak   Headdress set with silver coral, turquoise and other semi-precious stones, worn by the women of Ladakh.

Persian wheel   Method of raising irrigation water into a channel, by means of a rotating wheel, around whose perimeter clay pots are set at regular intervals.

phulkari   Shawls of *khaddar* cloth worked by Punjabi women in silk, leaving much of the background cloth unembroidered (literally, 'flower work').

pickling   The immersion in acidic solution of a piece of jewelry to clean off flux and oxides that still adhere to it after heating.

pietra dura   The Italian-derived technique whereby intricate floral designs in semi-precious stones are inlaid into white marble.

puja   Hindu prayer ceremony.

Rajput   A member of the ruling warrior caste to which most Hindu rulers belonged.

repoussé   The technique of 'pushing forward' the design from the back of a sheet of metal.

rezai   Padded quilt.

rudraksha   Seeds of the Javanese tree *Eleaocarpus ganitrus*, revered and used in India as beads for necklaces and rosaries by Shaivite priests, holy men and devotees.

Sanskrit   The language of the ancient Aryans, still used for religious rituals today.

shilpashastra   The ancient code governing the aesthetics of stone-carving.

shisham   A common type of wood used in the making of furniture and wooden printing blocks.

sindura   Painted or lacquered jars to hold *sindur*, the scarlet powder with which a married Hindu woman marks her parting.

surahi   Container for liquid, with a tall, thin neck.

sthapathi   Sculptors or architects.

Sudra   A caste category, low in the Hindu social scale.

tachardia lacca   The tree-dwelling insect which secretes lac, from which Indian lacquer is refined.

Tantra   Indian yogic system in which sexual and geometric symbolism play a major part.

tarkashi   The technique of inlaying thin ribbons of sheet brass into wood.

thali   Eating tray.

thanka   Tibetan Buddhist icon or mandala painted on cloth.

thewa   A technique involving the setting of silver wire covered in gold leaf into a softened layer of green glass or enamel, as a substitute for true enamelling.

Tie-dye   The resist technique of patterning cloth whereby little peaks of the cloth are tied off before dyeing, leaving a pattern of dots or lozenges in the original colour.

Toda   A tribe of pastoralists of the Nilgiri Hills, Tamil Nadu.

Vishwakarma   South-Indian caste of stone- and wood-carvers.

BIBLIOGRAPHY

Aditi, New Delhi 1982

Ali, Mrs Meer Hassan, *Observations on the Mussulmans of India,* Karachi, 1978

Archer, Mildred, *Indian Popular Painting,* London, 1977

Aryan, Subhashini, *Crafts of Himachal Pradesh,* Ahmedabad, 1993

Bagley, Peter, *The Encyclopedia of Jewellery Techniques,* London, 1986

Barnard, Nicholas, *Arts and Crafts of India,* London, 1993

Bernier, François, *Travels in the Mogul Empire,* London, reprint 1981

Beveridge, Annette, trans., *Babur-Nama (Memoirs of Babur),* Delhi, reprint 1989

Birdwood, G. C. M., *The Arts of India,* Calcutta, 1880, reprint 1988

Black, David, and Loveless, Clive, *The Unappreciated Dhurrie,* London, 1982

Blurton, T. Richard, *Hindu Art,* London, 1992

Brijbhushan, Jamila, *Masterpieces of Indian Jewellery,* Bombay, 1979

Burnard, Joyce, *Chintz and Cotton, India's Textile Gift to the World,* Kenthurst, Australia, 1994

Chattopadhyaya, Kamaladevi, *The Glory of Indian Handicrafts,* New Delhi, 1985

Cooper, Ilay, *Rajasthan: The Guide to Painted Towns of Shekhawati,* Churu, 1987

Crafts Council of India, *Archana, The Language of Symbols,* no date

Crafts Museum, *Indian Dolls and Toys,* New Delhi, 1968

Dalmia, Yashodhara, *The Painted World of the Warlis,* New Delhi, 1988

Dasgupta, Prodosh, *Temple Terracotta of Bengal,* New Delhi, 1971

Dhamija, Jasleen, *Indian Folk Arts and Crafts,* New Delhi, 1970

—, ed., *Crafts of Gujarat,* New York, 1985

Doshi, Saryu, *Tribal India: Ancestors, Gods and Spirits,* Bombay, 1992

Dowson, John, *A Classical Dictionary of Hindu Mythology and Religion,* Calcutta, 1982

Dubin, Lois Sherr, *The History of Beads from 30,000 BC to the Present,* London 1987

Elliot, David and Julia, *Gods of the Byways,* Museum of Modern Art, Oxford, 1982

Fisher, Nora, ed., *Mud, Mirror and Thread: Folk Traditions of Rural India,* Ahmedabad, 1993

Gillow, John, and Barnard, Nicholas, *Traditional Indian Textiles,* London, 1991

Gittinger, Mattiebelle, *Master Dyers to the World, Techniques and Trade in Early Indian Dyed Cotton Textiles,* Washington D.C., 1982

Government of Orissa, *Orissa: A Language of Handicrafts in Timeless Harmony*, New Delhi, no date

Government of India, *Indian Handicrafts*, 1968

Haider, Sajjad, *Tilework in Pakistan*, National Institute of Folk and Traditional Heritage, Islamabad, no date

Handbook for Travellers in India, Burma and Ceylon, London, 1933

Harle, J. C., *The Art and Architecture of the Indian Subcontinent*, Harmondsworth, 1968

Hendley, Thomas Holbein, *Indian Jewellery*, Delhi, 1991

Hitkari, S. S., *Phulkari, The Folk Art of Punjab*, New Delhi, 1980

Hussain, Javeed, 'Potter's Craft – A Pakistani Perspective', in *Journal of Pakistan Archaeologists Forum*, Vol. 1, Issue 1, June 1992

Huyler, Stephen P., *Village India*, New York, 1985

Jacobs, Julian, *The Nagas: Hill Peoples of Northeast India*, London, 1990

Jain, Jyotindra, *Folk Art and Culture of Gujarat*, India, 1980

—, and Aggarwala, Aarti, *National Handicrafts and Handlooms Museum*, New Delhi 1989

Jayakar, Pupul, *The Earthen Drum*, New Delhi, no date

Krishna, Nanditha, *Arts and Crafts of Tamil Nadu*, New York, 1992

Mashe, Jivya Soma and Mashe, Balu, *The Warlis, Tribal Paintings and Legends*, Bombay, no date

Michell, George, ed., *Living Wood. Sculptural Traditions of Southern India*, Bombay, 1992

Mohanty, Bijoy Chandra, *Patachitras of Orissa*, Ahmedabad 1980

Mukherjee, Meera, *Folk Metal Craft of Eastern India*, 1977

Murphy, Veronica and Crill, Rosemary, *Tie-dyed Textiles of India: Tradition and Trade*, London, 1991

Nabholz-Kartaschoff, Dr Marie-Louise, *Golden Sprays and Scarlet Flowers: Traditional Indian Textiles from the Museum of Ethnography, Basel, Switzerland*, Kyoto, no date

Narain, Brij and Sharma, Sri Ram, trans. and ed., *A Dutch Chronicle of Mughal India*, Lahore, 1978

Nicholson, Julia H., *Jainism: Art and Religion*, Leicester, 1987

Pathy, Dinanath, *Traditional Paintings of Orissa*, Bhubaneshwar, 1990

Raja Dinkar Kelkar Museum, *Treasures of Everyday Art*, Bombay, 1988

Ranjan, M.P., Iyer, N., and Pandya, G., *Bamboo and Cane Crafts of North East India*, New Delhi 1986

Rushbrook Williams, L.F., *The Black Hills: Kutch in History and Legend – A Study in Indian Local Loyalties*, Bhuj, 1981

Saraf, D. N., *Arts and Crafts of Jammu and Kashmir*, New Delhi, 1987

—, *Indian Crafts, Development and Potential*, New Delhi, 1982

Sen, Prabhas, *Crafts of West Bengal*, Ahmedabad, 1994

Shah, Haku, *Votive Terracottas of Gujarat*, New York 1985

—, *Form and Many Forms of Mother Clay*, New Delhi, 1985

Singh, Gurcharan, *Pottery in India*, New Delhi, 1979

Smith, John, *The Epic of Pabuji: A study, transcription and translation*, Cambridge, 1991

Stronge, Susan, *Bidri Ware Inlaid Metalwork from India*, London, 1985

Talbot Rice, David, *Islamic Art*, London, 1975

Thakur, Upendra, *Madhubani Painting*, India, no date

Turner, Eric, *Brass*, London, 1982

Vequad, Yves, *The Art of Mithila: Ceremonial Paintings from an Ancient Kingdom*, London 1977

Vitsaxis, Vassilis G., *Hindu Epics, Myths and Legends in Popular Illustrations*, Delhi, 1977

Von Leyden, Rudolph, *Ganjifa: The Playing Cards of India*, London, 1982

Wheeler, Sir Mortimer, *Civilizations of the Indus Valley and Beyond*, London, 1966

Whitechapel Art Gallery, *Arts of Bengal*, London, 1979

—, *Woven Air, The Muslim & Kantha Tradition of Bangladesh*, London, 1988

Yadov, Joravarsinh, *Folk Art and Culture of Gujarat*, Gandhinagar, 1992

Zaman, Niaz, *The Art of Kantha Embroidery*, Dhaka 1993

INDEX